Study programme

Block VIII Parts 1–4   Contents

The use of libraries and literature

D. J. Simpson and P. M. Smith

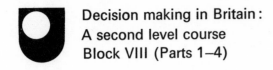

Decision making in Britain:
A second level course
Block VIII (Parts 1–4)

Patterns of decision making?

The Open University Press

Prepared for the Course Team by a working group comprising:

David J. Murray (Chairman)
Francis G. Castles
Ruth Finnegan
Carol Haslam
David Potter
Francis Sealey

The Open University Press
Walton Hall Bletchley Bucks

First published 1972
Copyright © 1972 The Open University

Designed by the Media Development Group of The Open University

Printed in Great Britain by
OXLEY PRESS LTD.
LONDON AND EDINBURGH

SBN 335 01948 X

This text forms part of the correspondence element of an Open University Second Level Course. The complete list of units in the course is given at the end of this text.

For general availability of supporting material referred to in this text, please write to the Director of Marketing, The Open University, Walton Hall, Bletchley, Buckinghamshire.

Further information on Open University courses may be obtained from the Admissions Office, The Open University, P.O. Box 48, Bletchley, Buckinghamshire.

1.1

Block VIII – Study Programme

Part	Course text	Television	Radio	Other material
1	Decision making in Britain – guidance on a synthesis	Programme 16 The Prime Minister as decision maker		
		Programme 17 The importance of Parliament		
2	Decision making – notes and essays		Programme 31 Them	The further material comprises the previous seven blocks of the course. There is no additional new reading.
			Programme 32 The Revolutionaries	
			Programme 33 The Reformers	
			Programme 34 A final review	
3	The social sciences and contributing disciplines			
4	Developing further the study of decision making in Britain			

Introduction

1 Block aims and objectives

The aim of this block is to assist you to come to conclusions on the major issues raised in this course. The central objective can be stated as being that at the end of this block you should have used the analyses of different sectors as a basis for considering different models of decision making in the arena of the whole society, and that in consequence you should have formulated conclusions about decision making in Britain. The first two parts in the block are devoted to this objective. Part 3 is designed to clarify the way in which the course has advanced an understanding both of contributing disciplines and of their interdependence in the context of the course, and thus at the end of Part 3 you should be able to explain the way the course has contributed to building up a knowledge of the social sciences and of the disciplines of economics, geography, political science and sociology. In the final part guidance is given on how to take further your study of decision making in Britain. The block has the general aim, therefore, of providing an opportunity for reflecting on the work done to this point, integrating the separate parts and making judgements.

2 The organization of the block

The block does not present new material. The subject matter for study is the material previously presented in the course. Obviously greater attention needs to be given to some parts of the course material than others, and the material in the Reader[1] has a particular importance; but it is the course material to which attention is directed in this block. There are no new set books, no dossier, no additional articles in this block, and the block text is there simply as a guide and stimulus in your work of synthesizing the material in the course and drawing conclusions from it.

Part 1 of the block contains two sections and two associated television programmes. Section 1 in the course text provides guidance on how to use the material in the course to achieve the major objective of the block. Section 2 draws together points about the use of sources. In so doing it provides a concluding note on one aspect of the second general course objective, that of developing skills of enquiry, investigation and comprehension. As the text makes clear, this has a close connection with Section 1 and with the work of making a synthesis of the material in the course.

The two television programmes are particularly associated with this first part of the block. Section 1 suggests that one way of approaching a reasoned conclusion about decision making in Britain is to start from the formal structure and ask how far an account drawing on this model needs to be modified or rejected in the light of the alternative models and of the way decision making actually operates. The two television programmes contribute here by taking two centrally important institutions in the formal structure – the office of Prime Minister and Parliament – and exploring how significant a part they play in practice in the decision making process.

---

1 Castles, F. G., Murray, D. J., and Potter, D. C. (eds.) (1971) *Decisions, Organizations and Society*, Harmondsworth, Penguin Books.

Part 2 of the block comprises a series of notes on previous blocks, a collection of short essays advancing particular opinions and the four radio programmes. This part is something of an experiment. It is conceived with the idea that reflection on what has gone before in the course will be stimulated by a series of short notes presenting provocative critical opinions from different standpoints. We recognize that, having worked your way through the previous seven blocks, you may be understandably reluctant to look again at the material and reflect on it, and that it will be even more difficult to look at it from a fresh perspective. We also know, as you do, from the returns recorded on the first CMA at the beginning of the course, where many of you stood in your initial assessment of decision making in Britain. We have, therefore, produced these notes and short essays as a stimulus to fresh thinking, and as a challenge to what may well by now be firmly held conclusions. They are there to provoke thought, and do not necessarily represent the personal judgements and conclusions of the authors. The notes were prepared, I should add, in the first place by F. G. Castles and D. C. Potter, and other members of the course team contributed additional notes. It is for you to put these notes and essays to whatever use you find convenient.

The essays also have a second aim, and that is to serve as examples of examination style essays. How convincing and how good they are is for you to judge. Those of you taking part in discussion groups may well find them useful as a basis for discussion.

The four radio programmes in the block are integral to the strategy of this second part. Each programme, like many of the notes, is designed to present a point of view or outlook which conflicts with, or challenges, conclusions you may have drawn. The programmes should prompt further questioning and encourage you to formulate judgements in a consciousness of problems and counter-arguments.

Part 3 of the block needs little explanation. Disciplinary themes were introduced in Block I, Part 4, and the notes on the disciplines in this part of the final block restate or develop points made at the beginning. To the notes on individual disciplines is added a short section on the course as a contribution, not simply to individual disciplines, but to the social sciences more generally.

The final part of the block is designed to assist you in achieving objective 1A in the general course objectives: to be equipped to continue your exploration of the topic of decision making in Britain beyond the point this course takes you. As the introduction to that part explains, there is no particular advantage in tackling it before the exams: it is there for you to use as you pursue further your investigations and enquiries.

3 Assignments

There is no TMA directly associated with this block. Time is technically allowed for completing TMA 10, but this TMA is one that is not necessarily immediately related to the block (the assignment was explained in the supplementary material in Block I), and many of you will have already completed and submitted it before receiving this block. Similarly there is no assessment CMA. In the supplementary material you will find the same schedule as appeared in CMA 41 at the beginning of the course. As on that occasion there is no requirement that you complete and return the form, but we very much hope that you will as it makes an important contribution to feedback. It will also be of interest to you to compare your interpretation at the end with that at the beginning.

While emphasizing that there is no Tutor- or Computer-marked Assignment with this block, it is important to stress that the work in this block is crucial to the course, and will necessarily be tested in the final examination. The final exam is concerned not simply with particular blocks, but with the course as a whole, and the work in this block is vital to the advancement of the general course objectives whose attainment will be assessed on the basis of the final examination. In terms of words to be read, and even more of new material to be mastered, this block is a small one, but in terms of work to be done it is big and most significant.

Part 1
Decision making in Britain – guidance on a synthesis

Section 1
Attaining the objectives of the course
David J. Murray

Section 2
The interpretation of sources
Ruth Finnegan

Part I Contents

Section 1
Attaining the objectives of the course

1   Introduction

In the first block of this course I set out and explained the course objectives. The objectives were expressed in general terms and related to different parts of the course, and the primary aim of this final block is to put in perspective the work that you have done so far. The first part of the block will indicate how the objectives have been covered so far and point out major questions that remain outstanding as you seek to put together the separate parts and achieve a synthesis around the central questions of, who makes the decisions that matter in Britain? where are these decisions made and by whom? what are the constraints? how far indeed are changes or developments the result of decisions that are consciously made?

The first block set out the general objectives for the course. These objectives have been developed, amplified and restated in succeeding blocks as each sector has been studied. In this block an overview of the course as a whole is being sought; as a start, the general course objectives will be recapitulated and the way they have been covered so far considered.

A checklist of general course objectives:

1   To gain some understanding of decision making in Britain, involving:

knowing what is involved in making decisions
comprehending characteristic features of decision making processes
understanding different interpretations of what are important decisions
knowing to a level to provide necessary context about contemporary governmental institutions and recent British history
understanding in some detail institutions and decision making processes in selected sectors
comprehending and applying, and analysing sectors on the basis of, four questions about decision making – namely:

What is the formal decision making structure – are decisions taken within this, and if so at what level, or are they taken within some informal structure? Who are the decision makers?

What are the constraints within which decision makers in Britain operate?

What are the effects of decisions and, in particular, how do these effects constrain future decisions?

analysing on the basis of models, synthesizing using them, and comprehending difficulties and limitations in the use of models
analysing possible differences between decision making in different sectors
using the analyses in different sectors as a basis for considering different models of decision making in the arena of the whole society.

1a   To become better equipped with the knowledge, abilities and skills required for formulating judgements about, and deepening knowledge of, decision making in society.

2   To develop skills of enquiry, investigation and comprehension and specifically to induce an informed, critical approach to source material of various kinds.

3   To advance understanding both of contributing disciplines and of their interdependence in the context of the course.

The course has been organized around general objective 1 above. It is this objective and the subordinate objectives listed under it which have determined the outline of the course and its coverage. After commenting on the other objectives, I will return to the relationship between particular parts of the course and the subordinate objectives listed under 1. It has been the aim to achieve objective 1a while working towards objective 1, for the idea behind this objective is that you should not stop giving thought to decision making processes in society or to characteristic features of British society at the end of this course, but rather go on to topics and issues that have been raised. Knowledge gained and skills acquired or practised are intended as a foundation on which you can build further. The second and third of the general course objectives have not structured the course. As explained in Block I the aim has been to achieve these objectives as the opportunity has arisen.

In this final block the first two parts are directed toward general objective 1, while the remaining parts take up the other objectives. The final part relates to objective 1a, providing some guidance on how you can proceed beyond the point attained in this course and undertake further investigation. A brief conclusion on objective 2 is included in Part 1, while Part 3 summarizes how the course has contributed to an understanding of contributing disciplines and of their interdependence.

The block as a whole is designed, therefore, to enable you to synthesize the material investigated in the course around the general course objectives. What is central to this work is considering the ground covered in Block I and in each of the sectoral blocks in relation to the basic questions about who makes the decisions that matter, where, within what constraints and with what effect. It is these questions which have dictated the subordinate objectives in general course objective 1, and which have structured the course. In the first block a basis was laid through acquiring knowledge about what is involved in making decisions, comprehending characteristic features of decision making processes and understanding different interpretations about what are important decisions. In the reading you did of D. Thomson, *England in the Twentieth Century*, and in *Britain: an Official Handbook*, but especially in A. H. Hanson and M. Walles, *Governing Britain*, you were laying the ground work for the investigation in the different sectors in a way that complemented the investigation of decision making and decision making processes; for this reading enabled you to gain a considerable knowledge of contemporary governmental institutions and of recent British history.

The next objectives in Objective 1 are those that have been pursued in the sectoral blocks. You have in Blocks II–VII been able to gain an understanding of institutions and decision making processes in these sectors, and in doing this various models have been deployed, and something done to draw attention to the differences between sectors. What these blocks have not aimed to do and what belongs peculiarly to this final block is to use the analyses in different sectors as a basis for considering different models of decision making in society as a whole.

It is, therefore, a major objective of this block that you should consider the investigations you undertook in each of the sectors covered by the previous blocks, reflect on the conclusions you came to about them, and then achieve a synthesis that provides you with some form of answer to the questions 'who makes the decisions that matter? where? within what constraints and with what effects?' So far questions have been asked, and much material investigated; it is now time for each one to formulate personal conclusions. It is the aim of the first two parts of this block to assist you to do this. What these parts will not do is to try to hand down conclusive answers. The reasons for this may well be evident to you already, and will be made clearer as you work through these first two parts of the final block.

In approaching the question of who makes the decisions that matter, and the other related and consequential questions, two different strategies can usefully be pursued. These two approaches were indicated in the succession of general course objectives and have been followed in each block of the course, beginning with Block I. One is to isolate important decisions, or decisions that matter, and having done so to proceed to discover the way those decisions were made. A second strategy is to identify the general features of the decision making process or processes in Britain, and on the basis of isolating this process or processes to draw conclusions about what belongs to the general category of important decisions, as well as about other interrelated questions concerning decision making in Britain.

2   Approaching a synthesis on the basis of important decisions

One way to identify any general decision making process in Britain, and thus to be in a position to answer questions about who makes the decisions that matter and so on, is to identify important decisions and to proceed from there to see how these decisions came to be made. Finding out how decisions were reached demands careful enquiry but it also depends on a consideration of what are important decisions.

In Part 2 of Block I there was an essay on decisions that matter which was intended to stimulate or provoke you into thinking out some of the problems involved in identifying such decisions. Two articles in the Reader (those by Bachrach and Baratz and by Dahl) also addressed themselves in part to this problem, and many of you will have been encouraged by your tutors to pursue your own thinking on this question. At this point I propose to review certain of the issues involved again, since, if you are to seek a synthesis about decision making on the basis of generalizations concerning the way important decisions are made, it is particularly important that you are clear about the basis on which you decide that one decision is an important one and another is not.

The problems involved in identifying an important decision – a decision that matters – are considerable. There are difficulties in the first place in deciding on what is a decision. On the face of it making a decision sounds like a single act by a single person. Can it also encompass collective activity? It is part of common speech to state that the electorate as a collective body decides – the British electorate decides that a change of government is needed; the Swiss electorate in a referendum decided to allow women the vote, and so on – and if it is valid to speak in this way of the electorate it is presumably equally valid to speak of other collectivities deciding, for example the miners deciding to go on strike. These are examples of collectivities choosing between alternatives at roughly the same time, but can decision making encompass group or organizational activity over time? R. G. S. Brown in the Reader described the way decision making is factorized in a British government department, and how something that emerges as a decision of a government department is the outcome of a whole range of lesser choices which, coming together, can amount to a major decision. Thus an initial choice concerns the issue of whether you will use decision making to describe simply an individual person's act of choice between alternatives, or whether you will use it to cover the action of groups or other collectivities. In this course the latter alternative has been followed, but you may devise good grounds for rejecting it.

A second set of difficulties concerns the delimitation of important decisions in the arena of the whole society. It is given that the course is concerned with British society as a whole and not with one person, one family or one parish, and thus the issue is how to determine what is a decision that matters in British society as a whole. An initial choice here lies between a personal definition of important decisions and what the society in some way treats as important decisions. Taking the first alternative involves formulating a personal definition or adopting someone else's. Bachrach and Baratz suggest a decision arising from a challenge to 'the predominant values or the established rules of the game', or Potter 'a choice with great consequences for persons in an arena of social relations'. Others, while not explicitly defining an important decision, do so implicitly. One example will both illustrate this and provide a contrast with the two previous definitions. For Hegel, to whose ideas some of you were introduced in Unit 2 of D100, what constituted an important decision in the arena of society was what he termed positive right or law. In Hegel's philosophy an individual could only exist as a part of a nation, with the state as the spiritual embodiment of the nation's will and destiny. What shaped the destiny of the nation and the state as an organic entity was a metaphysical force variously termed the spirit, mind or reason, and it was this that found expression in law. Yet what is a true expression of the spirit and what is the nature of this spirit is something that can only be understood through a study of history. Thus what is implied in Hegel's philosophy is that important decisions are the positive laws made by the state since these embody the spirit of the nation, but individual laws can only be appreciated as positive laws when viewed as part of the historical unfolding of the spirit of the nation over time.

This cursory exposition of an idea from the writings of Hegel provides a major contrast to the previous two definitions of an important decision, and it illustrates the point that any definition of an important decision depends on a particular philosophy. With the example of Hegel this stands out because the interpretation rests among other things on an organic theory of the state and on the existence of a metaphysical force – the spirit. With the other examples given above this foundation in a particular philosophy may be less obvious but it is there. At least it is evident that the philosophies reject certain Hegelian premises. The second example moreover depends on a philosophy which puts a greater value on change than on maintaining the status quo; it involves a value judgement that decisions that produce change are important and decisions that prevent change or maintain the status quo are unimportant. And the first example, while not proceeding so far, rests on a judgement that decisions in response to a challenge are more important than a decision which bolsters the status quo while not being taken in response to any challenge to the existing order. Whether, in other words, you formulate your own definition of an important decision or adopt someone else's the definition will involve a personal judgement and express personal preferences.

To the extent, moreover, that any such definition of importance is in terms of its effects there are problems about whether the effects to be considered are intended or unintended, direct or indirect. How far, in other words, are effects to be pursued before they can cease to be attributed to a particular decision? Was the death of thirteen people in Londonderry in January 1972 the result of the decisions of individuals in firing guns, of the officer in command in sending troops past the barricades, of the Civil Rights Association in holding an illegal march, of the decision by King James I to settle Ulster?

Finally, there is an important practical problem in using any definition of an important decision, even, that is, when you have established ground rules about how to handle effects. In so far as any definition of an important decision depends on the effects, however sophisticated the techniques used for assessing effects, it is problematical whether such a definition could apply to a decision in the immediate present. A colleague has expressed his judgement here as follows: 'important . . . is not a concept capable of being affixed to decisions as they are about to be made. The consequences intended by decisions about to be made may be important. Likewise, the intended consequences may be trivial: that again says nothing about the importance of the decision.' In assessing decisions in the immediate present, or in evaluating decisions about to be made, there is, therefore, the further issue of how far the effects or consequences can be predicted. Can this be done for all, can it be done for some, or can it be done, as Hegel's philosophy implied, only as part of the study of history?

The alternative to using some such definition of an important decision is to present an interpretation of what the society in question regards as important decisions. While this is obviously no easy task, there are nevertheless various indications that could be used such as coverage by the press or broadcasts, or opinion polls.

Finally, there are a range of problems about negative decisions and even more about non-decisions. An assessment that, for example, a decision taken in 1971–2 not to enter Europe would have been unimportant may derive from an individual definition of an important decision, from a limited definition of effects, or from a faulty judgement on results. At the same time it emphasizes how negative decisions can pose problems. One question to ask here is whether these can be overcome by re-expressing a negative decision as a positive decision. Any negative decision can be re-expressed in this way. A decision not to go into Europe is a decision to preserve Britain's independence from Europe; a decision not to intervene in Czechoslovakia in 1938 was a decision, among other things, to preserve peaceful relations with Germany. Maybe when re-expressed in this way such decisions can be encompassed within certain definitions of important decisions; they could, for instance, be covered by that of Bachrach and Baratz, since both the aforementioned instances would come within the category of responses to a challenge to the established order.

More difficult still is the point discussed in Bachrach and Baratz about non-decisions. The fact that some issues do not come forward for decisions to be made on them is itself most significant. The replacement of the present first-past-the-post electoral system in Britain by proportional representation is not an issue which either of the dominant parties allows to become a matter for decision or discussion – at least in relation to Britain. Some decisions are kept out of consideration both because of the way the decision making process is organized and because power is distributed in particular ways. When, therefore, important decisions that are made are isolated and generalizations produced about the process of decision making, it is still necessary to look again at the decision making process to ask how the process puts some issues out of court.

These then are significant issues that arise in approaching decision making through important decisions. The fact that there are such questions in no way invalidates this approach to finding answers about decision making in Britain. There are problems in determining what is an important decision and in determining how such a definition can be applied, and what is essential is that in formulating an interpretation of such decisions and working out how to use criteria established, there should be an awareness of the problems. Questions need to be asked and answers given, and in giving answers there is need of an awareness of how tentative they will be. This is not the place to be delving deeply into Hegelian philosophy or into logical positivism as a preliminary to investigating decision making in Britain, but it is relevant to be aware that a formulation of what is an important decision rests on philosophical and ethical assumptions. This subsection has taken you through certain questions that need to be considered in formulating your criteria for selecting important decisions. On p. 18 is a simple algorithm, setting out the alternatives explained in this section as a guide to making such a judgement.

Important decisions: an algorithm

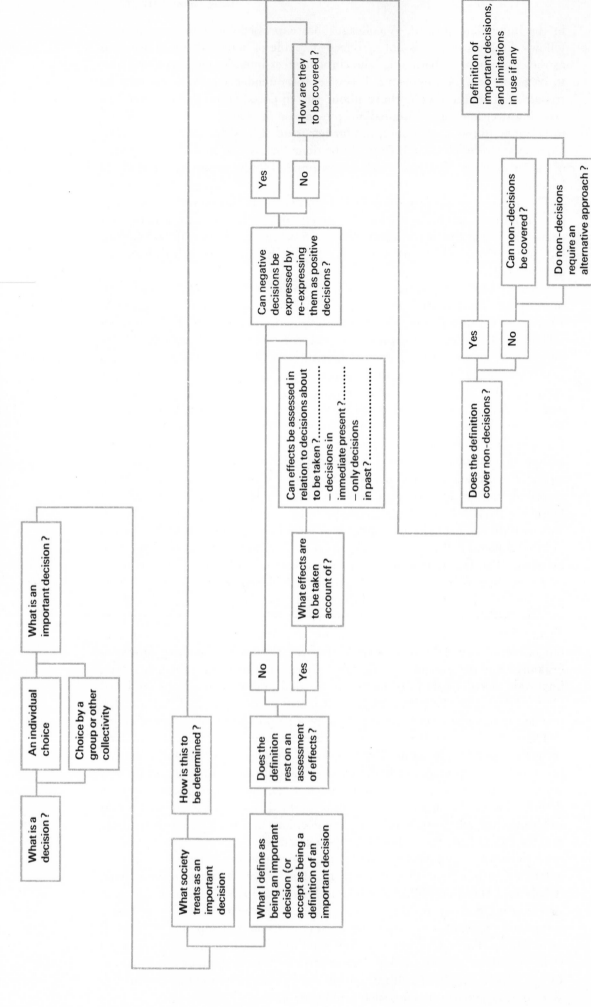

As implied in the previous paragraph there has, however, been a second reason for setting out certain of the issues and alternatives in dealing with what is a decision that matters in Britain. There can be no conclusive answer to what is a decision that matters. Any criteria selected for determining such a decision will reflect philosophical and ethical assumptions. For the course team to pretend that there is any objectively true answer would be to deceive you.

3   Generalizing about the decision making process

A second way of approaching an answer to those interrelated questions of who makes the decisions that matter, where, within what constraints and with what effects is to generalize about the decision making process in Britain. That is, instead of starting from the important decisions, and then seeing how these decisions were made, to begin instead by identifying the way or ways in which society is organized to make decisions. As the first block indicated the process of decision making in Britain comprises decision making units – individuals, groups, organizations – plus the regular patterns of interrelationship between them. A process, as one account puts it, is 'sets of interactions among components of a system' (Roberts, 1971, p. 176), and in this instance the components are individual decision makers and decision making institutions. Thus the second approach to a synthesis about decision making in Britain is to identify the components and the patterns of interrelationship that exist between them and see how these fit together in a general decision making process or processes in Britain. This is what was described in Block I as 'the building bricks approach'.

From your work in Block I you have built up an appreciation of decision making as a general process. That block concentrated on particular parts of the decision process – the characteristics of a decision; individual, group and organizational decision making, and the relationships which link together the individuals, groups and organizations into a process of decision making in societies; and in looking at relationships it gave particular attention to *influence*. The concern to identify the decision making process is a prelude to answering those questions about who make decisions that matter; and, as Dahl indicated in his critique of the ruling élite model (Reader, p. 354), this involves identifying who is able to influence whom. As the extract in the Reader by Gamson showed (Reader, p. 129), there are considerable difficulties in assessing influence, but for all its problems an attempt can be made. With the process distinguished, you can begin to explore answers to questions about where decisions are taken, about who commonly influences whom within the process, about the constraints imposed on different categories of decision makers, and about who characteristically make the decisions that matter in that they exercise a major or predominant influence within the decision making process.

This approach is to be distinguished from one utilizing important decisions (subsection 2). Making a synthesis on the basis of identifying regularities in the decision making process does not isolate important decisions, at least in the sense required under the first approach. In the first approach what was sought were criteria that could be applied to all decisions to determine whether they were important or not. Identifying a regular decision making process (or processes) will indicate that what emerges from that process belongs to a category of important decisions – important simply in the sense that they have emerged from the regular process – but unless it is assumed that all decisions are invariably made through a fixed process this cannot be an all-embracing definition of an important decision, as is needed in the first approach. For example if you identify Parliament as the focal point in the regular decision making process in Britain then, in terms of the process, decisions of Parliament (i.e. laws) are important decisions; but unless you assume that every decision is taken through this process, it does not follow that laws are the only important decisions. Unique or irregular decision making processes may throw up decisions like the Curragh Mutiny (Thomson, 1965, p. 32) or the Easter Rebellion (*ibid.* p. 55); these were not decisions of Parliament, and to deny their importance on the grounds that they did not emerge from the regular decision making process would highlight the shortcoming of such an interpretation of important decisions. The approach to a synthesis through the decision making process is not intended to proceed by a circuitous route through the stage of distinguishing important decisions; rather, the approach depends on the idea that by isolating a regular process, and studying its working, it is possible directly to explore the questions of who, where, within what constraints and with what effects? The process includes influence relationships and, by identifying these and observing their operation, the assumption is that it is possible to identify where predominant influence lies. In this way the important decision makers are those who can be identified as having this predominant influence: they make the decisions that matter in the sense that within the general decision making process of the society they are the ones who have the major effect on what emerges from the process.

To discover the characteristics of any general process (or processes) involves a consideration of what happens in British society. It requires an understanding to begin with of British political institutions and their background in recent British history. Block I, through the work on Thomson (1965) and Hanson and Walles (1970), was laying the ground for a consideration of the general process by which decisions are taken in different sectors of British society. Appreciating some of the issues and theoretical problems is only a prelude to the important task of finding out what goes on in Britain. Discovering about decision making in Britain is not an exercise in theory or logic chopping, though it requires clear thinking and a critical frame of mind; it also depends heavily on empirical investigations of what people and organizations in Britain do.

At this stage what is needed in terms of this approach is to draw together the conclusions you have come to about the working of British political institutions and of decision making in each of the sectors considered. In doing so you will be making a synthesis of your knowledge about the decision making process or processes in the arena of British society. How this task can be approached requires a consideration of the use of models.

This and the previous subsection therefore have been indicating how to approach the material in this course with the objective of answering those questions about decision making in Britain. This can be done both by isolating important decisions, seeing how these decisions were made, and then generalizing from this analysis to the regular decision making process, and, secondly, by identifying the regular process on the basis of a consideration of how individuals, groups and organizations commonly interrelate so that general patterns are discerned. Both approaches provide generalizations about the process of decision making and so allow for conclusions to be drawn about who makes decisions, where, within what constraints, and with what effects.

4   Employing models

In order to make a synthesis of the material covered in this course and formulate conclusions about the decision making process, you will probably find it desirable and necessary to make use of models of decision making in the arena of the whole society. Throughout the course models of decision making have been employed as a guide to enquiry. These models have differed in the use to which they have been put; some have been concerned with a particular aspect of decision making, such as the models of individuals as decision makers – the issue of whether for example they are most usefully regarded as maximizers or satisficers – others are applicable to the situation in society as a whole. Thus in each sectoral block an investigation has not only been made of decision making in a particular sector of British society, but the usefulness and validity of certain models has been explored. At this point certain of these same models can be used to assist in forming conclusions about decision making in society as a whole.

By this stage in the course you will be aware of the main models of decision making in societies used in the course. There are six principal models of decision making in the arena of society as a whole which have been introduced and it will be useful at this stage to recall these models and their main characteristics. In the first place, three models were introduced in Part 3 of the Reader: the ruling class, élitism, and pluralism. In Block II these models were supplemented by a formal structural model which was laid out in the context of decision making in public order in Britain, in Block IV a rational goal seeking model was used, and in Block V the issue was raised of whether the model of a negotiated order, there introduced in the context simply of a hospital, could be used in the arena of society as a whole.

Each of these is a model in the general sense explained in Block I, Part 4, as applying to models as used in this course. Each is a simplified representation of reality. The models are an abstraction drawn not from a single society, but formulated on the basis of the study of a number of situations or a number of societies. They provide a way of looking at a particular society, in that they give guidance on what to look for, and how to look at it. They use particular concepts, abstract certain features of society and postulate particular relationships. They encourage generalizations about a specific society on the basis of a study of the particular.

With the exception of the formal structural model, which is to be found in Part 2 of Block II, and the goal seeking model in Block IV, each of these models is explained in the Reader and, with the exception of the model on negotiated order, each is also criticized in other extracts in Part 3 of the Reader. Those who have not yet had time to study Part 3 of the Reader in particular will find it useful to do so at this stage, and it will be rewarding for all students to refer back to the material.

In looking at the exposition of these models, it is worth bearing in mind that while the models have features in common, they also have significant differences. First of all certain of the models are associated more obviously than others with normative theories about society. The models presented in Part 3 of the Reader are presented in the context not simply of what is, but what ought to be, and other contributions in that part challenge these normative theories: Playford, for example, exposes and criticizes the normative theories underlying various pluralist writings. Secondly, there are differences in what the models offer in terms of conclusions. A ruling class model, at least at a superficial level, points to answers on each of the questions of 'who makes decisions that matter?' 'where?' 'within what constraints?' and 'with what effects?' while others, as will be seen below, provide only more limited guidance.

Whatever their differences these models offer a way of looking at society and its decision making process, and also provide guidance on the questions with which this course is concerned. On the basis of conclusions about the general decision making process, further conclusions can be reached about who makes the decisions that matter, and where; they help towards an appreciation of constraints and in a measure with effects.

At this point it is appropriate to outline important characteristics of the six models.

(a) Ruling class

The organizing concepts in the Marxist version (as opposed to that of Mosca for example) are ruling class and subject classes. The ruling class is characterized by ownership and control of the means of production, and because of this the focus of attention is on economic power and the mastery of it. Through control over economic power the ruling class is able to control institutions of government; and government, or the state, is an instrument of the ruling class for furthering its ends. These and other instruments of control in society are employed by the ruling class to advance the self-interest of the class. Subject classes are those who neither own nor control means of production.

In terms of the questions in this course the model indicates the following answers: 'who make the decisions that matter?' – the ruling class; 'where?' – a question of possibly limited significance since wherever such decisions are stated (whether in a government institution or not) they derive from the self-interest of that class; 'within what constraints?' – dominant constraints are economic, connected with the ownership of the means of production; and 'with what effects?' – in the short term and put in very general terms the answer is the advancement of the self-interest of the class.

(b) Ruling élite

In this model an élite dominates the decision making processes in the society. This élite consists of a small number of persons, and may be drawn from a single subgroup in the society, for example the bureaucracy, or from several subgroups, such as big landowners, old Etonians and financial interests in the City of London. It is a characteristic of the élite that it is not representative of the community in social terms and generally is drawn from the middle and upper class. A ruling élite, however, is not simply that minority in the population that fills important offices, but a well defined group whose characteristics and membership can be specified. A ruling élite in controlling the machinery of government may, and it is often stated that it typically does, go through the form of democratic conduct, but in practice it will manipulate the process and will impose its will, excluding, if it so wishes, the influence of the rest of the community. The answer indicated therefore to 'who makes the decisions that matter?' is a ruling élite, for, whatever the apparent position, in practice the situation is manipulated by the ruling élite. 'Where?' – again within the ruling élite although the form may be followed of making decisions appear to emanate from the legal and formal institutions of government. No answer is implied on the constraints on the élite nor on effects; both are matters for empirical enquiry. It is not implicit that decisions are taken only in the interests of the élite.

(c) Pluralism

According to this model there is a socio-political system in which the power of the state is shared with a large number of private groups, interest organizations and individuals represented by such organizations. Political power is fragmented among the branches of government, and is moreover shared between the state and a multitude of private groups and individuals. Those in high places within the state may appear to have great power, but in reality they are only mediators among conflicting interests for whose power and support they must continuously bargain. In a measure the government and bureaucracy are to be viewed as disinterested umpires in the struggle among interest groups, and the power of private interest means that they often achieve their ends at the expense of the majority. In this model particular attention is directed towards interest groups and bargaining relationships. To the question of 'who?' the model directs attention towards no simple answer, but towards one that emphasizes the fragmentation of power and diffusion of decision making through different organizations in society – the particular situation being peculiar to each society. The answer to 'where?' lies in the answer to 'who?'; among constraints emphasis is placed on the constraints imposed by the need to bargain with a range of other interests who themselves have power within a political system where power is fragmented. The model makes no direct contribution towards an answer to 'what effects?'.

(d) Formal structural model

This model was introduced in the second block, where it was explained in the particular context of the maintenance of public order in Britain. Since then you have had the opportunity to follow elaborations of this model, particularly in *Britain: an Official Handbook* and, with qualifications, in Hanson and Walles (1970). In this model, the formal structure, comprising offices, institutions and procedures established under law and the constitution, are abstracted. It is within these that the important decisions are taken because they are prescribed under law and the constitution as being the decision making bodies for the society, and it is therefore on these that attention is necessarily concentrated. The formal structure prescribes and determines who makes the decisions that matter, and the answer to 'who?' therefore is the holder of a particular office to whom is assigned the responsibility and authority to take particular decisions. The answer is not Mr. X because he is a member of the ruling class or is the spokesman of the trade unions, but in his role of Cabinet Minister in virtue of the authority belonging to that office. In answer to 'where?' the model directs attention again to the formally established offices and institutions of the state. What is implied in this model of decision making is that a basic constraint is that decisions should accord with law and be taken according to the procedures prescribed by the law. Beyond this the model suggests no way of regarding or categorizing constraints. With regard to effects and to the way one decision constrains future decisions, the model directs attention to the ongoing effect of changes in the law and in formal institutional arrangements.

(e) Goal seeking model

The goal seeking model is one that was set out in the context of particular nationalized industries as a means of understanding and assessing decision making within these organizations. It is a model that has been widely used, in various forms, in the study of organizations, and its use has been extended to larger arenas, including sectors of society, and in a measure to society as a whole. In this course, besides its exposition and use in Block IV, a form of the model appeared in Block VII as part of the discussion of the national interest. In this model the critical concept is that of the goal, which is taken to mean a state of affairs which an organization – or society – is attempting to realize. In Parsons' language 'a goal is an image of a future state, which may or may not be brought about' (Parsons, 1937, p. 44), and in this model decision making is interpreted as the process which is directed towards the achievement of such a goal or goals. The significant activity is that action within an organization or society – depending on the unit being studied – which is directed towards the achievement of the stated goal or goals. In assessing the decision making process, it is frequently assumed that since activity is directed towards achieving the stated goal, decision making is concerned with how to utilize resources to the best effect. What this model abstracts, therefore, are first of all goals, secondly, behaviour directed towards the achievement of the goals, thirdly the decision makers as those who use resources in pursuit of the goals, and finally the conditions which affect the decision makers' choices. The model provides a particular way of looking at organizations, or a sector, or society, in that it directs attention to certain features in the situation and, in addition, commonly provides a criterion for assessing actual situations. In other words, it frequently has a strong normative element, saying that given a specific stated goal there is an 'efficient' way to act, and what is actually done is judged against this as a departure from what should be done. As a descriptive rather than a normative model, the model provides no direct guidance on who make decisions that matter, or where such decisions are made, but by delimiting the significant decision making activity as that related to the attainment of stated goals, it points a way to identifying the decision makers and their location. The model directs attention to begin with, therefore, to the question of what are the goals of the organization, sector or society, and points subsequently to the need to identify the means for achieving these goals, and hence both to the decision makers who utilized resources in pursuit of the goals and also to the conditions which affect their choice between alternatives.

(f) Negotiated order

The final general model of decision making is that introduced by Strauss and his associates and termed by them the negotiated order, which is elaborated and illustrated in their article in the Reader (pp. 103–23). The model was developed to help understand and explain the situation at the level of a hospital ward and of a hospital as a whole. It is not developed or elaborated as a model of decision making in society. The question has been raised previously, however, of whether the model can be extended and employed to understand decision making in the arena of society. Whether it is applied in this arena or in the more limited one of a hospital, the model shares certain of the basic assumptions of pluralism – notably that power in practice (rather than according to a legal theory of sovereignty) is fragmented. It goes on from this assumption to focus on the negotiations in society. It abstracts from a social situation, not the formal organization, or group organization, or classes, but interpersonal interaction and the patterns of agreement reached in this interaction. In this model the formal structure is one contributor, as is ideology, to the way individuals perceive and interpret situations. These factors therefore affect behaviour and decisions, but on the basis of individual perception. By extension, therefore, government is not a neutral arbiter, as postulated in a pluralist model, but a collection of individuals who are affected by their perception of the formal organization as are others, and what is important is the way this perception influences them in the negotiations they enter into. Besides directing attention to negotiation as a product of interpersonal interaction, the model places an emphasis on change. In abstracting from a social situation it does not postulate a stable order which undergoes changes, but predicates that a feature of social situations is that they are constantly in flux. As regards the answers put forward in this course the model directs attention to the possibility of all in a society playing an ongoing part in the decision making process: the answer to 'who?' is 'all'. What it does not provide guidance on is how to evaluate the relative significance of different individuals. It does not assume that all are equally influential, yet neither does it assist in defining different degrees of importance in moulding the total and constantly changing negotiated order. Similarly, to 'where?' the answer to which attention is directed is 'everywhere' but, in terms of which areas are more important than others, no guidance is provided. Regarding constraints much emphasis is necessarily placed both on the constraints imposed by individual perception, on the fragmentation of power, and on the need for a process of bargaining and negotiation. In a sense the effects of an individual decision are built into the model in that emphasis is placed on the way social order is constantly changing and every decision is affecting that order.

These models should help you in your work of making a synthesis of the material covered in the course. In the first place they can assist with organizing the ideas derived from a consideration of how important decisions are made. During the course case studies have been presented of a series of decisions, and these as well as others derived from your own further reading and direct experience provide a basis for your consideration first of whether they are important decisions, and, secondly, of the way they were made. As a reminder I will run through the main case studies considered in this course.

Block I. The Labour government's decision not to proceed with its industrial relations legislation (TV Programme 1 and correspondence text Part 1).
The Conservative government's industrial relations legislation (Radio Programme 4).

Block II. A decision by a juvenile court on boys in trouble (TV Programme 3).
The decisions by policemen at the Garden House Hotel, Cambridge (Radio Programme 6).

Block III. Annual price reviews (set book, Self and Storing).

Block IV. The Fuel Policy White Paper (correspondence text Part 5 and TV Programme 8).
Railway electrification (correspondence text Part 6 and TV Programme 9).

Block V. The creation of the National Health Service (set book, Willcocks).

Block VI. The decision to raise the bank rate (set book, Chapman).
The Warwick Sunday Market (Radio Programme 25).

Block VII. The decisions on the sale of arms to South Africa (correspondence text Part 6 and TV Programmes 14, 15).

Taking whichever of these you regard as important decisions, together with others also derived from your wider experience and other reading it is for you to consider the process by which the decisions were made. In doing this the different models outlined above can provide you with guidance on what to look for, how to look at the situations, how to organize the details of each episode and how to formulate generalizations about decision making processes in Britain. One use of the models considered in this course therefore is in helping you to come to conclusions about specific decisions introduced in this course.

A second use is in the other approach to making a synthesis outlined above. The second alternative was to concentrate on the regular process or processes of decision making in Britain. In making a synthesis of the course around the question of the regular decision making process or processes, one way to exploit models is in the manner followed in the different sectors: that is to start from the formal structure of government and to question the validity of an interpretation that assigns the decision making process to this structure, and explore the situation on the basis of alternative models. In Block II, for example, the block started from the formal structure and went on to point to limitations in the idea, expressed in the formal structural model, that all important decisions on public order are taken by the legislature and responsible ministers as provided by the law and constitution. The general approach of starting from this formal decision making structure has been followed in each sectoral block and indeed was provided for in the objectives of the course, one of which was 'comprehending and applying four questions about decision making and analysing sectors on the basis of them – namely what is the formal decision making structure, are decisions taken within this . . .?', and given this approach in the course you will find it most straightforward in drawing your conclusions to start from a formal structural model of decision making.

If you begin from the formal structure of decision making in Britain – guided by the formal structural model – it will then be appropriate to reflect on the adequacy of this as a convincing interpretation. It will be necessary to consider the extent to which, if at all, decision making regarded in this way in Britain requires elaborating, qualifying or modifying, or whether indeed this picture of decision making in Britain should not be wholly rejected, and in asking questions the alternative models will suggest questions to ask, alternative organizing concepts to use, and different ways of looking at the situation. Such questions as the following are suggested:

Although major decisions appear to emanate from the formal structure, being expressed as laws or decisions of the Cabinet, are these in fact simply the instruments of a ruling class, or are these institutions in practice being manipulated by a ruling élite, 'the establishment'?

Do such decisions within the formal structure represent the agreements achieved between competing interest groups, with Cabinet and legislature providing formal confirmation?

Should the assumptions of a stable, almost static order be wholly rejected in favour of one which sees the whole process in a constant state of flux?

These are only examples of the questions that need to be asked and explored. The alternative models provide guidance on questions to ask and on how to formulate an overall picture of the decision making process in Britain, and in consequence draw conclusions about who makes decisions that matter, where, within what constraints and with what effects. When you have come to your conclusions in this way you will be in a position to compare these with the ones reached on the basis of considering the way important decisions were made. Each strategy will result in conclusions on the same topic though each, as subsections 2 and 3 above indicated, are unlikely to be complete. An approach through important decisions leaves unexplored the area of non-decisions; the approach through the decision making process leaves unattended decisions which do not emerge from the regular decision making process (or processes). Where, therefore, there is a discrepancy between the conclusions you draw on the basis of the two approaches, it needs to be asked why this difference arises and whether it derives from the limitations in the two approaches.

5   Conclusion

This section is intended as a guide in your work of revising the course and coming to conclusions on the questions posed for the course. To make a synthesis of the material in this course around these questions involves:

1   Determining what you will treat as an important decision.
2   Selecting from the cases studied in the course or outside it those decisions you regard as important.
3   Generalizing about the process by which those decisions were made.
4   Considering the decision making process in Britain, starting with an identification of the formal decision making process.
5   Assessing the strengths and shortcomings of an interpretation that represents decisions as being made as provided by the formal structure.
6   Forming conclusions about the way to represent the decision making process in Britain.
7   Comparing the conclusions derived from the first strategy with those from the second.

References

Britain: an Official Handbook (current ed.) London, HMSO.

CASTLES, F. G., MURRAY, D. J., and POTTER, D. C. (eds.) (1971) *Decisions, Organizations and Society*, Harmondsworth, Penguin Books (the Reader).

HANSON, A. H. and WALLES, M. (1970) *Governing Britain*, London, Fontana.

PARSONS, T. (1937) *The Structure of Social Action*, New York, McGraw-Hill.

ROBERTS, G. K. (1971) *A Dictionary of Political Analysis*, London, Longmans.

THOMSON, D. (1965) *England in the Twentieth Century*, Harmondsworth, Penguin Books.

Section 2
The interpretation of sources

Before reading this section spend a few minutes asking yourself how far and in what respects you have achieved course objective 2 (the part relating to an informed critical approach to source material).

This section provides some concluding comments on the source criticism aspect of objective 2 of the course. But though there are some points I wish to add or re-emphasize at this stage, I do not intend to present any elaborate or comprehensive conclusion. This is for the two reasons (1) that what matters is *the skill you yourself have been exercising and developing* and lengthy academic cogitations or exhortations from me at this point are not going to contribute much to that one way or another; and (2) that most of what I would wish to say is already expressed in the earlier section on the critical use of sources (Block I, pp. 129 ff.) and there is no point in merely repeating that here; rather, you will find it useful to look again at that earlier section and its accompanying exercises in the light of the work you have now done throughout the course. Thus, though the general topic is an important one in the course, the points that I wish to elaborate in this conclusion can be treated fairly briefly.

First, I want to draw your attention to the progress you have undoubtedly made in your capacity to use sources, in particular sources concerned with contemporary Britain. This progress is something you may not yourself be fully aware of, and may indeed doubt. This is particularly likely because of the way in which exercises specifically directed to the source criticism objective in the first two blocks or so were replaced in later blocks by different kinds of assignments and exercises in which the source criticism aspect was not so explicitly stressed.

It is probably worth recalling some of the ways in which you have been exercising and developing the skills of using sources during this course.

The items specifically designed by course team members or consultants to elucidate this aspect were perhaps less important than the places where you were actually using sources for yourself. But even these items had relevance not only for providing information but also insofar as you too participated in the analyses involved. So it is worth mentioning, for example, the introductory section discussing the question of using sources (Block I, pp. 129 ff.); the second television programme ('Television as a source'), which analysed the first one from the point of view of source criticism and included some penetrating comments from Stuart Hall, both in the programme and in the accompanying notes, on some characteristics of television as a source; the ninth radio programme, which suggested some of the possible points to bear in mind when interpreting interviews, with illustrations mainly from programmes previously broadcast in the course;[1] and Radio Programme 19, on interpreting an interview.

There were also a whole series of points in the course at which the source criticism aspect was implicitly touched on or exploited. You will easily be able to extend this list for yourself, but some examples include: Radio Programme 10, in which Peter Self answered questions about the composition and contents of

---

1   Some of the same points are also re-emphasized in James Barber's introduction to the interviews with John Boyd-Carpenter and Richard Crossman in Television Programme 15 and in the note for Radio Programme 31.

his book (Self and Storing, 1962, one of the set books); the notes for Television Programme 7, where you were invited to compare the text of the full interview as contrasted to its edited version in the programme; Radio Programme 14, which discussed the validity and problems of the questionnaire for the CMA in Block I; the notes accompanying certain broadcast programmes in Block V (e.g. the television programme on ideologies) where you were given guidance in making your own interpretation of the material presented there; and the guidance in Block I, Part 3 on approaching the background reading. Block VI is of particular importance because here you were engaged not only in evaluating and criticizing source material of various kinds, but also in facing some of the problems of collecting material. In one sense you were learning about and experiencing the process of creating certain source material and seeing how certain sources could 'come into existence' (as it was put in the introductory source criticism paper, Block I, pp. 142 ff.). In another sense you were going directly to what could be called one of the most primary sources of all: the actual people whom you interviewed. Some of the Block VI correspondence material discussed precisely the problems and complications arising from conducting and using interviews as source material (see particularly the discussion by A. Bates on pp. 43 ff. about the problems of validity and reliability, etc.). This block is therefore a significant one for the whole question of how one interprets sources, and thus makes a crucial contribution to the source criticism objective of the course as a whole.

However, helpful as some may have found such direct or indirect discussions by academics of problems to do with source criticism, the opportunities in the course for you to engage in actual practice of the skill of source criticism for yourself will probably have been even more significant. In the earlier blocks there were easily identifiable exercises to give you such practice (e.g. the exercises in Block I (pp. 149 ff.) on various topics to do with Britain,[1] in Block II (pp. 195 ff.) on passages relating to the police, and in Block III (p. 110) on interpreting statistical sources. There were also two optional TMAs set in Block I specifically to do with criticizing sources (TMA 01 (4) and TMA 10 (1)). It may not, however, have been so immediately obvious that later blocks too included many opportunities designed wholly or partly to give you practice in using and developing your source criticism skill, in ways which built on the relatively more straightforward exercises in earlier blocks. In Block III, for instance, you were required as part of your work to go through the dossier of various different kinds of source material relating to agriculture in Britain and your TMA built on this. In Block V, the process of testing and evaluating the hypothesis about regional disparities in the health sector (Part 2) involved one aspect of interpreting and making use of source material. Block VI was notable for giving you practice both in analysing and interpreting source material in a relatively large-scale synthesis (leading to a double TMA) and in participating in the process of actually collecting source material with the necessity of evaluating and making decisions in this context too. Block VII presented somewhat similar opportunities to Block III in giving you a set of documents (in this case accompanied by television) as source material which had to be analysed and interpreted as part of the work for the block TMA. All in all you will have worked through many exercises and assignments in the course which specifically gave you practice in developing your skill in assessing sources, whether or not the objective was explicitly spelt out in each case.

More than this, analysing and interpreting source material is something you will have been engaged in not just in specific assignments, etc., related to

---

1   NB. If you have not yet completed the first exercise there (described on pp. 138 and 149) you may find it helpful to do it now as part of the revision process.

objective 2 but throughout the whole course. Reading through set books and deciding, for example, to make notes or not to make notes on specific sections; studying sections by course team members and consultants in the correspondence material and concluding that, say, you agreed or disagreed with certain bits or found them illuminating/unilluminating or slanted in one direction or another; deciding to skip certain parts as irrelevant; following up some further references as of particular interest and not others; interpreting odd items in newspapers, broadcasts or conversations as pertinent to certain questions in the course – all these are ways of exercising critical skills on source material. Again, with certain broadcast programmes (e.g. some of those in the agriculture and health blocks) you will have been actively involved in interpreting source material which has sometimes been presented to you in a deliberately undigested form. In these and similar ways you will have been developing your skill of assessing sources throughout the course, even when you were not fully conscious of doing so. There is a sense in which, particularly as one progresses, this skill is no longer in practice a separate and discrete thing, but a necessary element in the intelligent study of any subject.

Therefore, provided you have worked reasonably systematically through the course, your skill in assessing sources will certainly have developed and been exploited during your work for this course. Obviously it is a skill that you (like all of us) will continue to develop further still. It is something clearly of the utmost use in many different contexts – not only in further university courses. Though in the end it emerges as something which in a sense is just a way of reading or observing intelligently, and not really something that can be practised on its own and in isolation, nevertheless if you do wish to make a *deliberate* effort to cultivate it further it might be worth occasionally setting yourself a specific source criticism exercise, similar to those in the course; another very effective way of reinforcing and developing a skill like this is to consider how you might teach it to someone else, and even try actually teaching it. But in any case you would be justified, as you end this course, in feeling confident that you have made some progress in the skill of assessing source material. It is worth stressing this, for, though it is the actual *practice* of a skill that matters most, being aware of this and reflecting on it sometimes helps one to deploy it even more effectively.

So much for the first point I wished to emphasize. The second point concerns the increased knowledge you have now acquired through the course about British institutions and British society. This turns out in fact to be exceedingly pertinent to the source criticism objective of the course. As it was put in the introductory paper on source criticism, one of the first principles about using sources is: 'Consult as many of the relevant sources for a subject as you can – or (put another way) the more you know about a subject already the better you can assess and criticize the source relating to it' (Block I, p. 137). Thus the fact that you now know so much more about the general background, about what type of sources there are and the implications of each, and about the kind of assumptions likely to be made on various issues – all this puts you in a position to use and interpret sources on contemporary Britain that much more knowledgeably and effectively. Thus the work you have done in relation to objective 1 of the course will in fact have contributed to your achieving of the objective relating to the critical use of sources (course objective 2). Indeed the more you learn about Britain over the years the better equipped you will be in this respect to deploy your skill of assessing source material relating to Britain.

This leads on to my third point. This is the relationship of the source criticism objective to course objective 1a which, as you will recall, runs: 'To become better equipped with the knowledge, abilities and skills required for formulating judgements about, and deepening knowledge of, decision making in society' (Block I, p. 128). This is an objective of central importance to our conception of the course even though it is obviously not one that is easy either to give specific instructions about or test directly in an examination. But your increasing skill in dealing with source material in a critical and informed spirit should certainly contribute towards your achieving this objective. The most important aspect here is probably your actual practice in exercising this skill, but one should also remember that *information* about sources and their background can play a significant part. Here you will be helped, if you wish, say, to pursue some topic on contemporary Britain further than in the course itself, by the summary of types of sources for contemporary and recent Britain in Block I (Appendix 2 to Part 4, Section 2, pp. 147–8), by the bibliographic notes appended to various sections (e.g. Block II, pp. 127–8 and 194), and by the bibliographical advice in this block (Part 4 below), as well, of course, as by your increased knowledge of British institutions generally. Thus as far as the informed use of sources goes, you will certainly be better equipped now than at the start of the course for taking further your study of decision making and/or of Britain – whether you wish to do this just for interest, in connection with your job, or in some further university course. In this sense, the final test of this course should not lie just with the examination results at the end of the year, but in your interests and questionings over many years to come in both work and leisure. To this, the emphasis on interpreting sources in this course should certainly have made a contribution.

I have one final point to stress. This is the way in which the emphasis in the course has increasingly been on the 'interpretation' rather than just the 'criticism' of sources – that is, not on what might seem the destructive aspect of merely criticizing them, but on the constructive use to which they can be put. A parallel development in the course has been the increasing realization that to many questions about decision making in Britain there is not an agreed and single response that one would authoritatively give as 'the right answer'. To a large extent one's assessment of the answers depends on one's interpretation of the sources – and this interpretation in its turn depends on one's assumptions and even on the model(s) by which one is impressed. One's response to the course, therefore, should not consist just of learning off its content, but essentially involves an act (or acts) of subjective interpretation. Whether or in what sense this implies the impossibility of ever achieving 'objectivity' in the social sciences is a controversy that should be mentioned but cannot be pursued here.[1] However it would probably not be disputed by the majority of social scientists that one's conclusions must ultimately depend on one's interpretation of the evidence, in other words on one's assessment of the sources. This indeed must be very obvious not only from the somewhat different lines taken by different academics throughout the course, but also by the disagreements (which have deliberately not been concealed) in this block. When it came to trying to give overall answers to the central questions about the course, different people interpreted the evidence in different ways – just as you too will inevitably have been coming to your own conclusions on the basis of *your* interpretation of the sources. These differences in interpretation do not necessarily extend to *every* aspect of the subject – we are not just left with intellectual anarchy, for there are topics on which there is general agreement or on which at least certain groups of people tend to agree. But it would be wrong to conceal that there are (perhaps even should be?) disagreements based on different interpretations of the material.

---

1 If, as we hope, there is a 'Philosophy of the social sciences' course in the future, this controversy will doubtless receive full attention there.

There are many reasons for such differing interpretations (some discussed in the earlier paper, in Block I), but one in particular must be mentioned here. This is the effect of differing *models* on interpreting sources. If, say, one uses a Marxist model then certain aspects will seem particularly illuminating, important or convincing, and this will radically affect the final interpretation of the sources. Similarly with someone who relies on, say, a formal structural, or an élitist, or a pluralist model. Thus an awareness of possible models (one's own, other analysts', and those of authors of source material) becomes crucial in one's evaluation of evidence. For in this sense too the 'facts' are not self-evident, but depend on one's model when looking at them. In this way the objective referring to analysing in terms of models (one aspect of course objective 1 – see Block I, p. 128) turns out to be intimately related to that concerning the use and interpretation of sources.

The main conclusion that one can perhaps draw from all this is that many of the objectives laid down for the course at the start are more closely related than might have at first appeared. In Block I they may have seemed bitty and unconnected, but by now their relationship (even sometimes overlap) with each other is increasingly marked. Opinions will of course differ as to which, if any, of these objectives should be given first importance. I myself would suggest that the one concerning the interpretation of source material (objective 2) is perhaps the central one – in the sense at least that it should have helped to equip you with the skill to apply your mind and energies not only to the extremely important content of this course but also to areas and topics which the academics on this course may never have needed to think about.

Reference

SELF, P. and STORING, H. J. (1962) *The State and the Farmer*, London, Allen and Unwin.

Acknowledgements

Grateful acknowledgement is made to the following sources for material used in this part:

Longmans for G. K. ROBERTS, *A Dictionary of Political Analysis*; McGraw-Hill for T. PARSONS, *The Structure of Social Action*.

Part 2
Decision making – notes and essays

Part 2   Contents

Section 1
Notes

1   Introduction

As Part 1 of this block has demonstrated, our study in the *Decision making in Britain* course allows us to come to certain broadly based conclusions about the processes by which decisions are reached in this country. This does not, however, imply that the end of the course is the time at which to stop putting questions. In Block I a number of very important issues and questions were raised, to which students should have been referring back throughout their studies. Having now completed our substantive study, the time has come to look back to those issues and questions, to re-examine the course material in terms of them, and to see the extent to which (a) we have reached sensible conclusions, and (b) we must ask additional and/or more sophisticated questions if we are fully to understand the decision making process.

In Block I, four crucial questions were asked. They were:

1   What is the formal decision making structure – are decisions taken within this, and if so at what level, or are they taken within some informal structure?
2   Who are the decision makers?
3   What are the constraints within which decision makers in Britain operate?
4   What are the effects of decisions and in particular how do these effects constrain future decisions?

In addition, two further issues were raised in Block I which have implicitly or explicitly been raised time and again in the course. First, it was noted that to explore decision making at all it was necessary to distinguish between decisions that matter and others which do not. Second, it was suggested that an understanding of decision making could best be facilitated by examining the various models which purport to illuminate that process.

It is to these four questions and two major issues that we wish to turn our attention in this part of Block VIII. By somewhat reformulating these basic course themes, we hope to offer you a means by which you can assess for yourselves the degree to which the course offers a key to understanding decision making in Britain. Part 2 is devoted to looking at the entire course in terms of four questions, which encompass these basic themes of the course.

They are:

1   What are the most important constraints on decision making in Britain?
      This question combines questions 3 and 4 of Block I. As well as outlining the constraints under which decision makers in Britain operate it highlights the role of past decisions as constraints on subsequent decision making activity. Furthermore, by highlighting the 'most important constraints', it leads us to ask whether we can extract any generalizations from our study as to the major determinants of decision making in Britain.
2   Who are the most important decision makers in Britain?
      This obviously covers question 2 in Block I, but, again, by stressing the 'most important decision makers', it leads us to general conclusions about participation in decision making processes.
3   What are the important decisions?
      This question closely parallels the concerns expressed in Block I, Part 2,

'Decisions that matter', and raised again in Part 1 of this block, and is designed so that we may examine the contribution of the course to understanding the nature of the distinction between important/unimportant decisions in a British context.

4 What models are most useful for an understanding of decision making in Britain?

This question takes up the issue of models, and asks us to concentrate on their respective contributions to understanding decision making in Britain.

A student who has completed the course up to this point is likely to realize that it is impossible for the authors of this piece to come to definitive conclusions on wide-ranging questions like these. Because, however, we wish to avoid any suggestion of definitive answers, we have deliberately chosen a broken-up note format rather than the completeness implied by the essay form. The notes which follow are intended to be the authors' reflections on these difficult questions, taking up points from the various blocks insofar as they appear to be relevant. In reading these notes the student is not intended to be a passive spectator. His objective should be to come to his own conclusions on each of the separate questions, conclusions which may be as like or unlike the authors' as the evidence appears to warrant. Indeed, coming at this point in the final block, these notes may be useful to the student as a method for facilitating his revision.

The following notes are distinguished between those contributed by Francis G. Castles and David Potter, and those by other members of the course team. The latter are identified by ~~being printed in green and~~ the initials of the authors ~~are given.~~ These are as follows: J. Barber, A. Blowers, R. Finnegan, J. Melling, D. J. Murray, L. Power, R. Thomas.

2 What are the most important constraints on decision making in Britain?

2.1 Block I – Decision making in Britain: an introduction

As is appropriate for an introduction, the question: what are the important constraints? is raised in Block I but not answered there; and apart from general points there are only concrete illustrations here and there of constraints, e.g. that Eden was inhibited 'by the attitudes of the US State Department, by a Commonwealth alarmed at the idea of war and worried by the thought of a blocked canal, by the House of Commons opposition, even by hostile sections of his own government.

Every day he put off the decision a little longer.' Both the example and the general comments in Block I serve, as it were, to announce a trend sustained through subsequent blocks of being satisfied to list different types of constraints (from the very general 'economic forces' to the highly specific 'the attitudes of the US State Department') without distinguishing between them or suggesting ways of measuring the degree of intensity of one constraint as opposed to another.

The question of constraints also arises in the required reading for Block I, particularly that in the Reader. Audley, for example, ('What, makes up a mind?') suggests in effect that the important constraints on how someone makes a decision lie in his *previous history*: 'minds quite often come already made up' (Reader, p. 65); R. G. S. Brown ('The administrative process in Britain: decisions') speaks of the constraints on one's

options, because of *selective perception* in the *identification of a problem* as needing a decision at all (e.g. Reader, p. 90, cf. also Lindblom in Reader, pp. 28 ff) and of the constraints involved from the decision maker's *organization* (e.g. Reader, pp. 97 ff, also H. Brown in Block I, pp. 73 ff); a maximizing model like that criticized by Simon ('Theories of decision making in economics and behavioural science') would imply that the constraints lie not primarily in the decision maker's previous history or his perceptions, but in the *objective environment* – in the actual *utility* of possible decisions (Reader, pp. 40–1); for Strauss *et al.* ('The hospital and its negotiated order') the main constraints on decision making seem to lie not in the external environment or formal structure but in the constant and continual *negotiations* which, in turn, 'breed further negotiations' (Reader, p. 112); and so on, depending on how exactly the different analysts define the decision making process.

Some of this analysis, admittedly, focuses on constraints on individual *decision makers*, and is not specifically related to the arena of the whole society; nevertheless, since at least some of the important decisions affecting Britain are normally accepted as in some sense made by individuals, the question of constraints on individual decision making is relevant here. Further, the whole Reader discussion brings home the point that how one identifies 'constraints' depends on how one identifies the 'decision process', so that discovering the important constraints must to some extent involve a *judgement* about the nature of the decision process.   R. F.

Thomson (1965) embodies an interpretation of events in which the present, to be understood, must be seen in the context of history; the past constrains what can be done in the present, for 'even such cataclysmic events as world slumps and world wars do not totally divert or disperse the strongest currents of historical change'.

Hanson and Walles (1970) provide an interpretation of constraints which can usefully be contrasted with Thomson, emphasizing as they do the importance of tradition and past development but adding also a stress on the way the institutional structure imposes significant constraints and raising the question of the effect of these time constraints – and in particular whether the working of these constraints so hampers adaptation to new circumstances that the existing system of government will not be able to accommodate the accelerating pace of change in British and international society.   D. J. M.

2.2   Block II – Public order

This block is most explicit about constraints on decision making in the general area of public order. In particular, Part 3, Section 1 and Section 4, lead to a categorization of types of constraint; *viz.* ideological and background constraints. One useful exercise might be to see how well this categorization fits in other blocks.

One very important question which emerges from the treatment of the constraints which affect the decision making of the judiciary and police is the respective weighting of different contributory factors. What the block seems to provide is a checklist of the most important factors related to the maintenance of public order, but, apart from the use of linguistic comparisons (e.g. x seems more important than y – note that specific statements are quite hard to find in the block), there is no attempt to assess the importance of one factor compared to another. (Almost certainly this is also the situation in other blocks. This leads to two interesting reflections:

(a) That in a complex social situation the only exact technique for weighting the differential contribution of different influences or constraints might be factor analysis. That the impossibility of quantification in many social fields (public order among them) means that the best one can

hope for is a reasoned argument suggesting reasons for giving one factor more weight than another.

(b) Students are frequently surprised that there is not a determinate answer to many problems in the social sciences. The problem of assigning a weight to the multitude of factors which unquestionably affect a decision may offer one good reason why intelligent analysis may lead to disparate conclusions about decision making. For instance, two knowledgeable commentators on the way decisions are made in respect of public order might well answer the following question very differently: Of the many factors which affect decision making in the sphere of public order, which do you think are *most* crucial?

This block raises another very important issue in respect of constraints relating to the way that the models predominant in the minds of decision makers can act as very important constraints on their action. (See Part 5, Section 4, 'What model for analysing decision making in public order?') This is, of course, a point also made by Power in talking of ideological constraints. In either case, it seems that this could be a lead in to a conclusion which seems likely to emerge from the course as a whole: that it is not merely analysts who use models, but all social participants. Only by constructing a picture of reality is it possible to select among the many features of a situation relevant to making a decision, but that picture of reality may in a sense pre-determine what is found in the situation (this, of course, is the same 'chicken and egg' problem described by Finnegan in talking of the way the police 'create' crime).

The somewhat shadowy treatment of the formal structure as a constraint raises the problem of measuring the effect of negative constraints. At various points, Palley, Power and Finnegan note that judges and policemen are limited in their area of freedom to decide by the formal rules within which they operate (see the con-cluding section of Palley's essay in Part 3). But if a judge or a policeman decide that they *cannot* do something because there are formal rules or conventions preventing them, how can one know? Obviously, this point is likely to arise in other blocks. It does, however, seem to relate to what I felt to be the major difficulty with this block; that the importance of the formal structural model was dismissed with too little evidence.

In the two television programmes 'Children in trouble', although constraints are not *weighted* an attempt is made to *categorize* them in the implementation of a particular piece of legislation as follows: (a) constraints specified in legislation; (b) constraints agreed as rules within an organization (in this case the police); (c) constraints which develop from specialist training (dealing with juvenile offenders); (d) constraints which develop from the individual perception of the decision makers.

An important point which emerges from this categorization is that, while the exercise of discretion and decision making is constrained at all these levels, statute law when it is specific takes precedence. The other constraints operate within the framework of the law, which is sometimes tight and sometimes loose. This conclusion gives more support to the importance of the formal structural model than the statement in the note above which says 'the importance of the formal structural model was dismissed with too little evidence'. The 'evidence' which emerges from 'Children in trouble' is that the formal decision making model *helps* to explain decision making within the law, but to understand the full process we must go outside the limits of the model.

J. B.

Both Palley and Power were concerned to prove two different hypotheses in the Public Order block. First, that the process of interpreting the formal code of law was not a simple mechanical one, and second that discretion was necessarily built into the act of interpretation. Most of Palley's and a good part of Power's piece was devoted to this concern. If anything the point is over-laboured. The formal struc-tural model is certainly not immediately dismissed.

Our second concern was to show how important the formal code was in con-straining judicial behaviour – how belief in the need to appear impartial meant that conformity to the formal code became one of the judiciary's most important role considerations. In that sense, the judiciary continually assess cases in the light of a multitude of considerations while bearing in mind that their judgement must be justifiable in the light of the formal code – a code which is remarkable for its flexibility, not its rigidity. One cannot *know* in any absolute sense what causes a judge to make a decision. One can only generalize from his behaviour patterns as we have done in the Public Order block. But that of course is the basic problem of social investigation and not one which is specific to the understand-ing of judicial behaviour.   L. P.

2.3   Block III – Agriculture

A large number of constraints are mentioned. Innovative decisions by individual farmers or groups of farmers are discussed by Jones (Part 2) in terms of constraints which he groups under the broad headings of situa-tional, personal, psychological, sociological, and macro-environmental characteristics. Cheshire (Part 3) and Bowers (Part 4) in their analyses of national policy decisions refer to political ideologies and societal goals as constraints on decision making.

And Walters (Part 5) refers to the decision making structure itself as an important constraint. Such constraints could be listed indefinitely, where seemingly everything is relevant and in some way influences the decision outcome. This consideration sug-gests two general points: (1) it is important to define what is meant by constraint, a concept which has variable definitions; the concept is used loosely in this block and not defined there. (2) There is a close interconnection between identification of constraints and the particular model used in analysis; one model of decision making would highlight certain constraints, another model would highlight others.

An example of the latter point is the somewhat different way in which the notion of constraint is used in the essay by Walters. He raises a standard question from interest group theory: what are the reasons for the NFU's success or failure in pressing its demands on local and national decision makers? The question calls forth answers which can be defined as constraints, but which are of a rather different nature from those mentioned above, e.g. the extent to which decision makers, in acceding to pressure group demand, are helped or hindered in their work, or the degree to which the pressure group controls information resources available to decision makers. If instead of asking what are the constraints? one asks rather more pointedly about reasons for success or failure, then one gets a different list of constraints. Either way, though, the problem of weighting the factors or constraints remains, and is not attempted in this block for the same reasons as suggested in the notes on Block II.

An interesting distinction among environmental constraints can be detected in Jones's essay. He recognizes that variations in the physical environment provide an overall framework within which innovative decisions are taken. But it is changes in the non-physical environment – technological, economic, social and political – which explain the pattern of innovation diffusion. Such a distinction between constraints which set the limits of decision making and those which motivate individual decisions does not define which constraints are most important, though it can make discussion of that issue more explicit.   A. B.

This block also has quite a lot to say about decision consequences, for example: government policy encourages shift to capital intensive farming which in turn leads to declining labour force in agriculture and damage to countryside. There is no explicit treatment of decision effects as constraints on subsequent decisions in the block. But the point is implicit throughout the block, especially in Cheshire and Bowers, and cause-effect-cause chains of this sort can be constructed from the material presented in the block.

2.4   Block IV – Nationalized industries

Part 2, 'The decision to nationalize' points up two sorts of constraints which are either new to the course or have been dealt with in a rather different way:

(a) The historical dimension. The stress in the essay is on seeing current developments as the result of an historical process. By looking at the past one is able to achieve a more reliable perspective than by relying completely on the statements of contemporary commentators.

(b) The role of ideas. Previously (in Block II) we have talked about the way in which ideas can act as an implicit ideology affecting behaviour. Here the essay stresses the explicit role of ideology, but notes that, nonetheless, official statements of ideas cannot necessarily be taken at face value.

All the components of the block place a special emphasis on the role of economic factors as the determinant of decisions. 'The decision to nationalize' notes the importance of economic factors in the initial move toward public ownership. Part 3, 'The economic operations of the nationalized industries', stresses the complicated considerations which influence the decisions regarding what to produce, how to produce it, how much to produce, and what price and rate of return to achieve.

However, despite its emphasis on the economic, it is arguable that the major contribution the block makes in discussing constraints is its emphasis that in respect of any *important* decision, however purely economic in nature, non-economic considerations are bound to affect the eventual outcome This theme is clearly developed in Part 5, 'A case study of fuel policy', where the social impact of major unemployment is seen to have influenced government policy. It is discussed in rather more abstract terms in Part 7, 'The goals of the nationalized industries', where it is implicitly suggested that the need to consider non-economic criteria of social cost is one of the important factors in increased governmental intervention in the decision making process in the twentieth century.

In this block the point is also made that constraints can be deliberately constructed as a means by which one decision maker sets the operating parameters for a lower level decision maker. This is manifested in both:

(a) The nationalized industries' public accountability to the House of Commons.

(b) The economic and financial objectives, which are limits set by the government

within which the nationalized boards can make their decisions.

An interesting question about constraints is raised by Stewart's point in Part 6 about commuter subsidy levels being determined by factors extrinsic to the transport industry. The actual level of government support for any given sector may be determined by factors quite external to that sector. Is it arguable that an emphasis on sectors may lead to a neglect of those factors which set the parameters of decision making for all sectors?

In the section on power stations (Part 5, Section 4) Blowers deals with the constraints affecting a locational pattern. Three aspects merit attention. One is the importance of *time* constraints especially in an integrated power supply system. Marginal generating capacity has to be fitted into the inherited system based upon past decisions and must anticipate the future pattern of the system.

A second aspect of constraints discussed here is the relevance of spatial scale in decision making (see also Note on the health sector, below). Broad locational strategy which takes into account questions of fuel type or transmission technology is concerned with decisions at a macrospatial (national or regional) scale. The microspatial (local) scale becomes important when specific

locations are considered and here questions of water supply, site conditions, or amenity damage are crucial.

Thirdly, there is the question of *political* constraints. The government defines the area within which the CEGB is free to operate and can also determine locational decisions either directly or indirectly, through its fuel policy. At a local level decisions may be affected by formal or informal political processes.

Note how variations in the physical environment (distribution of coal, water supply, visual amenity) play an important part in determining the locational pattern. In Block III (see Note above) the constraining role of the physical environment was inferred, here it is explored.   A. B.

Finally, the block by its emphasis on goals and impacts implies the additional constraint of consideration of time future. Not only is the point raised that decision makers are influenced by what they intend to achieve, and what they think a given

policy will achieve, but it is further suggested that the extension of planning, and with it the development of social cost benefit analysis, is dependent on the most meticulous analysis of the likely by-products of any given decision.

2.5   Block V – Health

Part 3, Section 2, 'Welfare state and welfare society', illustrates another instance of the way in which the models in which men believe constrain their decision making activity. To those who believe in the 'public burden model of welfare' all welfare payments are a burden on the economy which

it is the object of a good government to remove. Not only does the model imply a selectivist social service policy, but it creates a state of mind which is unable to see some payments as a legitimate response to social welfare costs.

Geographical or spatial constraints also enter into the sphere of decision making in health (see Block V, Part 2). At the very least the implementation of a decision to, say, improve the health of people in the

north would be constrained in certain respects by the facts of the present geographical distribution both of disease and of health provision   R. F.

Part 4, Section 1, 'The doctors: interests in conflict', discusses an area of constraint which is presumably operative in all fields

in which there is government activity and intervention. Decision making in a particular sector, where it involves considerable expenditure, depends crucially on the relationship of the particular Ministry with the Treasury, and the extent to which the Cabinet as a body feels the Ministry's bid is justified in connection with other claims made upon the Exchequer.

The point noted by Willcocks, that the secrecy surrounding governmental decision making often makes it impossible for the scholar to know the exact nature of the operative constraints, obviously applies in varying degree to all aspects of the course. Some aspects of decision making are literally unknowable. Willcocks, like Gamson in the Reader, seems to feel that the resources a group possesses are a key to its power potential. Thus in considering the likely outcome of any negotiation between a number of groups one needs to consider:

(a) The respective bargaining weapons of the groups involved. In the case of health: skills, administrative machinery, property, consumer status and voter role.

(b) The bargaining weapons of the government. In the case of health: monopoly employer or paymaster.

2.6   Block VI – Business

Gamson argues (Reader, Part 2) that constraint, like inducement and persuasion, is a species of influence – one of several procedures for influencing a decision. Influence, he says, defined in terms of *net* effects, aims at (a) changes in a situation and/or (b) changes in the intentions of persons in that situation independently of situational changes. But what precisely is constraint? The note on p. 38 urges the need for precise understanding here. Gamson assists understanding by distinguishing constraint from persuasion and inducement. If influence is restricted to changes of the sort mentioned in (b) above, the influence is limited to persuasion. If influence extends to changes of the sort mentioned in (a) above, and contributes a facility or resource to the individual or group influenced, inducement has occurred. But if the influence changes a situation by removing a facility from an individual or group influenced, constraint has occurred. Gamson adds – if I understand him correctly – that persuasions never, and inducements always, imply the modification of situations through the influencer's control of a relevant facility.

Using these definitions, how can the 'hypothesis' or one part of the total 'hypothesis' with which Block VI is concerned be restated with a view to seeing whether it could be operationalized? We would begin, of course, by specifying which particular part of the 'hypothesis' we were to be concerned with, viz. that central government, business corporations, and the trade unions – three separate yet closely interrelated clusters of power – 'make, or are in a position to influence greatly, all major economic and political decisions' on the basis of an implicit consensus and of their acceptance of 'the values and imperatives of a modern industrial order'. Then we would go on to ask whether the alternative but not synonymous expressions, 'making decisions' and 'influencing decisions greatly', suggest the need to separate out the respective influence-potentials of government, business corporations, and trade unions. In other words, we would ask in turn of each of these clusters of power if they – 'are in a position to influence greatly all major economic and political decisions' on the basis of an implicit consensus and of their acceptance of 'the values and imperatives of a modern industrial order'. Then we would go on to ask in what way we could best separate out the respective influence-potentials of government, business corporations, and trade unions. In other words, we would ask in turn, of each of these power clusters, whether in its interactions with the other two it worked by constraint and/or inducement and/or persuasion.

To be useful, this enquiry would need to be tied to several particular issues. One example might be the CBI's Price Restraint Agreement of 1971. Whose initiative underlay the agreement – the CBI's, the TUC's, the government's, some other body's? By what methods – persuasion, inducement, constraint – was the agreement reached? Did the agreement modify the situation or did it leave the situation unchanged? If the agreement was itself the result of influence, did the agreement in its turn aim at influence? What, in any case, was the situation which the agreement sought to modify? Were there in fact different denotations for the term 'situation' when we asked the question as to the changes or otherwise which the agreement sought to produce in it? Was there a situation, in the first place, of such and such a rate of price inflation and, in the second place, of such and such a level of demanded wage-increases? And before answering whether the agreement exercised influence, would we not need to link the questions 'of what' and 'on whom' – and, conditionally at least, 'by what methods'?

With data on all these points, we could

ask whether they begin to provide an answer to the power-relations of these great institutions – between themselves and within society.

This would be only a 'first go' at approaching the task of verifying the original complex statement. That we would be on to a significant enquiry is suggested *prima facie* in the following remarks by Peter Jay, Economics Editor of *The Business Times* (May 1, 1971): 'During the Conservative government's first 300 days of mini-budget and budget, of the Industrial Relations Bill and public sector de-escalation, of surging cost-inflation and rising unemployment, consensus economic policies negotiated with the Trades Union Congress and the Confederation of British Industry were inevitably at a discount.' More interesting still is the statement in the same issue by John Davies, Secretary of State for Trade and Industry, that when he served as Director General of the CBI his position was 'a highly political one' and 'I had my eyes wide open to what the problems of Parliament were . . . I was very much confronted with the problems of government and industry day by day, and I suppose the thing that prompted my desire to go into the political field was that, in the

end, one stopped short of being the decisive force.'

In this connection, one wonders how the appropriate Railwaymen's Unions and Vic Feather, general secretary of the TUC, *really* responded to the Chancellor of the Exchequer's 'industrial blackmail' speech of 13 April 1972, delivered with the full approval of the government. In view too of the government's and CBI's known concern for price restraints, one wonders how Michael Clapham, deputy chairman of Britain's biggest chemical combine and the CBI's new president, is being influenced by the clash between the chemical industry's aversion to a fresh Price Restraint Agreement and the support of most CBI members for a renewed agreement. As a result will the whole chemical industry have to minimize its price increases? And will the expected response of the relevant trade unions to any increased profits in the industry serve as another influence?

These are only some of the questions that bubble up when influence and its several forms are considered in relation to business. Block VI has not been able to do more than touch at a single point the manifold issues presented by decision making in this sector.

J. M.

2.7   Block VII – External relations

As discussed in previous blocks, constraints are identified and discussed throughout this block, although they are not always labelled as such. For example, the point is made by Vital that each British government, on accession to power, finds itself confronted 'by a great accumulation of established practice and doctrine among their officials and of undertakings, arrangements and

Constraints can also arise from activity *outside* the state. This includes not only constraints through actions by foreign states, but also those that are outside the

Here and there in the block attempts are made to classify in some way the manifold constraints mentioned. Northedge (Part 5), for example, suggests a distinction between 'systemic' and 'idiosyncratic' forces, the former referring to constraints on foreign policy decision making *external* to the particular country making the decision, and the latter referring to *internal* constraints. Furthermore, as regards systemic forces, he distinguishes between (a) pressures deriving from the very nature of the international system of states, and (b) pressures deriving from the prevailing 'state of play' within

continuing conflicts which they have the greatest difficulty in ignoring or circumventing even where they are judged irrelevant to major governments purposes'. Almost everything that goes on within a state, from political party rivalry to the game of ping-pong, has a bearing it seems, on foreign policy making.

framework of the state altogether, in particular constraints due to the activities of multinational corporations.   R. F.

that system. But these interesting distinctions are not deployed consistently throughout the block (no criticism is intended here of this particular block; all blocks, and the course as a whole for that matter, suffer from this defect).

What might be termed 'incipient constraints' are referred to in an interesting way by Barber in Part 3, Section 1, 'The concept of the national interest and decision making in foreign policy'. His point is that on most items of foreign policy the general public 'lie dormant' but that they can 'spring to life' on certain issues. This possibility is constantly in the minds of foreign policy decision makers, and can be said to operate as a kind of constraint upon their actions.

There is an additional point made by Northedge of interest not only for this block but for the course as a whole. It is, quite simply, that to study recent or contemporary decisions like entry to the EEC

or sales of arms to South Africa suffers from the major drawback of lack of access to official documents. Thus, we are not in a very useful position to perceive many of the considerations (including constraints) which affected the decision. This can, of course, bias our findings, or even make our understanding of decision making and of particular decisions just plain wrong.

The above note rightly refers to Northedge's point that official documents are often not available. Northedge also says that evidence about direct personal contacts – the telephone conversation, the chat in the corridor – is unavailable. This raises an interesting question. Are there certain constraints in operation which decision makers would not record? For example, if a man, although good at his job, was not given promotion because, among other things, he was unpopular or had personal habits which were disliked, would this be recorded or would the written reasons not include this?

In such a case written records could be deceiving. Another aspect of recording decisions and the reasons for them is that in writing them down we might try to be more rational and give more specific reasons than had in fact been the case: i.e., we might try to rationalize our behaviour as we recorded it.

One of the television programmes specifically deals with constraints related to the sale of arms to South Africa. Among the questions raised in the programme are: (a) Is policy first conceived and then an attempt made to push it through despite constraints, or is it in fact directly shaped by the constraints (i.e., the decision makers attempt to find a route through the constraints which they perceive)? (b) How are constraints conceived? Are they, for example, seen differently by Labour and Conservative governments? If they are not perceived differently, is this because constraints are 'objective' and not dependent on 'subjective' perception, or does it rather indicate a wide consensus of perception among British policy makers? (The paper by Holsti and Northedge's radio broadcast both examine aspects of these questions.)

J. B.

2.8   Conclusion

By this point you should have reached some conclusions about question 1, 'What are the most important constraints on decision making in Britain?' and, most important, you should have made up your mind about the extent to which it is answerable at all. As the preceding notes indicate, it seems probable that the ability to reach an answer, and the nature of the answer itself, depend on a number of factors, of which the following three are probably the most important:

1   The amount of information with which you have been presented. The *Decision making in Britain* course has offered you a great deal of information about the constraints operative in the decision making sphere. Obviously, however, much more is available, both about the sectors you have already studied and about the areas which fall outside the competence of the course. Some guidance is given at the end of this block on how to undertake a literature search and thus widen your information, but what is certain is that the more information you acquire the more likely it

is that your conclusions in respect of this question will change and/or become more sophisticated.

2   The way in which you weight the different constraints which appear to be operative in the field of decision making in Britain. One of the things which stands out most clearly from the course is that the number of different constraints operating is virtually limitless. At the same time, it is quite clear that some times of constraints are more important than others – as a crude example, economic constraints have been mentioned more frequently than aesthetic ones – and one's overall answer to the question depends very closely on the weighting one gives one factor rather than another. Furthermore, it should be added that a consideration of the weighting of factors may of itself lead to the rejection of the appropriateness of the question. Perhaps it is impossible to talk about 'the most important constraints on decision making in Britain', because in the different sectors the respective weighting of factors is entirely different. Thus, it might be that the only

appropriate question would take the form: What are the most important constraints on decision making in the public order sector, in education, in defence planning? – and so on.

3 The standpoint from which you view the information that has been provided by the course. As the preceding notes make clear, the way you look at the existing data on factors which constrain decision makers depends both upon the model you are using and upon your accumulated personal experience of the system of decision making in Britain (the latter being a kind of implicit model you keep in the back of your mind). The weighting you attach to particular factors is likely to depend very much on the implicit or explicit models you bring to bear on the material contained in the course. Because all three factors are

interdependent it is perfectly possible for intelligent commentators on decision making in Britain to come to widely divergent conclusions on the question of what are the most important constraints. The commentators' information may be equally extensive and valid, but vary considerably, and the weights they attach to different constraints and the models they utilize may all be different. What is important is not that the question be always answered in the same way, but that you constantly search for new information, whilst simultaneously attempting to evaluate the arguments put forward for weighting factors in different ways and likewise keeping a sufficiently open mind to appreciate the varying insights that different models can provide.

3   Who are the most important decision makers in Britain?

3.1   Block I – Decision making in Britain: an introduction

Two approaches to identifying the important decision makers are introduced in Part 2 of Block I and in the reading that is integral with that part, and these are particularly relevant to the above question. First there is the approach through the decision making process and secondly that through decisions that matter. The part points to the need to identify the decision making process. It represents this as comprising individuals, groups and organizations which are themselves decision making bodies and which as decision making units in the society characteristically interact with each other. The regular patterns of inter-

action between these units can be characterized as the decision making process of the society. The assumption is that there are characteristic sets of interrelationship among components regarded as decision making units, and that having formulated generalizations about these sets of interrelations and thus constructed an account of the decision making process, conclusions can be drawn about who are the decision makers. The alternative approach starting from important decisions involves sorting out the problems about what is an important decision.

D. J. M.

When this question is first raised explicitly in Block I, it is prefaced with the remark that 'on the face of it, this is a straightforward question' once the decision making structure, formal and informal, has been accurately described. This formulation sets the trend for treatment in subsequent blocks, wherein much more attention is given to describing and analysing decision making structures in some detail, rather than trying to locate an individual decision maker.

However, earlier in the block, this latter type of exercise is suggested as appropriate when the point is made that John Anderson, Harold Wilson, and Anthony Eden can each be described as making decisions. A single person, it appears, can make a decision affecting the whole society.

There is, furthermore, a third level or type of answer suggested in Block I. This

is found in each of the three extracts which serve as case studies. In the panegyric to John Anderson, to the question of who are the decision makers the answer appears to be the War Cabinet – a handful of men. In the industrial relations piece (Part 1, Section 2), Vic Feather is described as declaring before supine TUC delegates the unanimous acceptance by the TUC of the 'solemn and binding undertaking'; and it is clearly suggested that very few people were directly involved in the decision to drop the proposed legislation. To the question of who made the decision to intervene in Suez, in the third case study, the answer is that the decision was made in a shelter beneath the River Thames by thirty British and French officers, plus the Prime Minister, the Queen, and their French counterparts.

So it turns out that an individual, or

thirty-four people in private, or a whole structure involving many people can 'make a decision' affecting all of Britain. Or, in a somewhat separate formulation, a ruling class, or an élite, or a plurality of competing and co-operating groups in Britain can make a decision, a threefold distinction also introduced in this block. In short, one's answer to the question of who makes a decision will be determined to some extent by the type of decision examined and the way it is looked at (i.e., by one's model). For example, it is not particularly surprising when, in examining a case study of a particular decision like the Industrial Relations Bill, one finds that a few identifiable persons are directly involved in 'making the decision'. Nor should we be surprised that when one looks at a set of decisions in a fairly loosely defined sector of British society one tends to find a structure of roles and interacting groups 'making the decisions'. In other words, the answer to the question of who make(s) the decision(s) is governed in part by the type(s) of decision(s) being analysed. One problem here is that no typology of decisions is given in Block I, apart from a crude distinction between important and unimportant decisions.

These considerations suggest the further point to the question of who is the decision maker that a student's answer is governed in part by the level or type of analysis being employed. To say, for example, that Anthony Eden alone made the decision on Suez is one possible answer to the question of 'who?' at a strictly formal level of analysis. But it is an answer of only very marginal interest or usefulness. To say that thirty-odd people interacting in a hole in the ground in London made the decision is another answer at another level of analysis – call it group dynamics in a face-to-face situation. And to say that persons, groups, perhaps the whole electorate outside that underground room also made that decision, even though they didn't know of its existence at the instant of choice, could also be an answer to the question at another level of analysis. And so on. This is an instance of how closely connected are this question and question 4, 'What models are most useful for an understanding of decision making in Britain?' in this concluding note about models.

Another, closely related point, which follows easily from what has just been said, is that answers to the question of 'who?' are governed in part by the way the student defines the notion of 'making a decision'. Although the following question is put succinctly in Block I: 'What is a decision and what does making it mean?' no answer to it is suggested in the block beyond identifying stages in what is called a process of decision making. But there are a host of problematic issues here. Is making a decision making a choice? (Yes: 'A decision occurs when a choice is made between alternative courses.') If so, then this definition encourages the answer that the decision being analysed was made by an individual. 'Making a decision may sound on the face of it like a single act but different stages in the basic process can be distinguished' (Reader, p. 15). In this alternative formulation, making a decision involves engaging in a process of behaviour with certain identifiable stages. If this is accepted, then this definition strongly encourages the answer that the decision being analysed is made by a number of people. Other ways of handling the notion of making a decision could also be suggested, each with a different bearing on the question of 'who?' This all comes down in the end to the simple point that the student's answer to the question of who makes the decision will depend mainly on the way he defines the concepts contained in the question itself. And, of course, in the absence of explicit definitions, which are not provided in Block I, students are bound to come up with variable answers to identical questions.

Another, somewhat separate point is made by Stacey in Part 3, Section 2. Under the Heath administration, it is stated that central government decision making has increasingly become a 'closed system' with decisions increasingly arrived at privately and the whole system of decision making in government more 'managerial' than 'participatory'. This assertion could, of course, be used to support an argument that decision making in Britain is increasingly élitist in character. Stacey's point can be kept in reserve until we know whether additional élitist conclusions are found in subsequent blocks.

Part 3 of Block I presents two extended statements of the decision making process in Britain. Hanson and Walles (1970) provides an account of the patterns of interrelationship and thus of the process of decision making which is fundamental to the course. The book is, as it says, a guide book to political institutions and in reflect-

ing on the rest of the course three questions seem particularly relevant; first, how far and in what way should the account of the patterns of interaction between political institutions be modified; secondly, what does this guide leave out of account; and finally, what does the description tell us about who makes the important decisions?

Is it a reasonable summary that it supports a pluralist interpretation to the extent that it stresses the importance and power of interest groups, but rejects any idea that the government is a disinterested arbiter between competing interest groups, treating those who occupy positions within government as major decision makers within the process?

The second statement of the decision making process comes in *Britain: an Official Handbook*. This sets out with clarity and detail a formal structural interpretation. It provides, therefore, an interpretation against which that of Hanson and Walles can be set and also one that can be assessed in succeeding blocks.   D. J. M.

3.2   Block II – Public order

This block offers clear evidence for the view that decision making power is widely diffused in the public order sector. This is the conclusion of Finnegan's 'What model for analysing decision making in public order?', Part 5, Section 4. It is illustrated throughout the block by showing (a) that the judiciary make decisions (Palley and Power, Part 3), (b) that the police make decisions (Finnegan, Part 4, Section 6), and (c) that public opinion has a major influence on decision making. Some of the ways in which the police negotiate with their clients make the point very nicely.

This block also offers clear evidence for

the view that decision making is centralized and concentrated in few hands. Power shows very clearly that the judiciary taken as a whole constitutes an élite group. Moreover, without ever mentioning that it is so, Palley's subsection on 'English judges and their role' (pp. 62–72) uses only examples of judges in the House of Lords or the appellate courts. This is very obviously a tiny sub-élite of the élite.

So quite different conclusions can be drawn from the evidence advanced in the block, depending on which evidence is selected.

The above note suggesting that different conclusions can be drawn from the evidence advanced in the block requires amplification. What I think emerges from the block is that there is a wide range of people involved in decision making within the law – judges, magistrates, police, probation officers, headmasters, etc. The range of decisions and discretion they exercise is in part formally laid down by law, but within the law there is a range of discretion which, among other things, is influenced by the functional role of the decision maker, the social morals within which he/she works and the individual's perception of his/her role. Looking across the range of the decision makers tends to give a pluralistic view of decision making, but looking at a particular group, e.g. the judges, tends to give an élitist view.   J. B.

Another possible approach is to point out that, though there is some possible evidence to suggest that *judges* may form an élite (see Block II, pp. 92 ff, 119 ff, 124), judges are only one section of the judiciary as a whole, and not *necessarily* the section which includes the most important decision makers in the sphere of public order. Williams states clearly that 'the vast majority of trials for crimes of public order take place before magistrates' courts. This reflects the traditional involvement of justices of the peace in the preservation of the Queen's Peace'

(Block II, p. 33). Similarly Palley makes clear that 'when the judicial statistics are examined it is obvious that it is the lower courts, staffed by the less distinguished members of the judiciary, which are charged with making most decisions and which have more direct impact upon the public' (Block II, p. 57). To be certain therefore that 'the judiciary taken as a whole constitute an élite group' (above), particularly as far as concerns decision making in the sphere of public order, one would also need evidence about the background and activities of these 'lower' members of the judiciary. It is not enough just to produce evidence about the more visible section made up by the judges or to depend wholly on the more easily accessible and quotable pronouncements by judges in the higher courts. Evidence about magistrates, etc., is not so easily available; less research has been undertaken at this level, though the 'assumption' is made that they tend to be 'conservative and middle class' (Block II, p. 123). The question must therefore to some extent be left open – with the qualification that, on the face of it, it seems not very likely that all (or most) magistrates, etc., together with the judges, can really all be classed together in a single decision making élite.

The related question then arises of which decisions (and hence which decision makers) are more important in the sphere of public

48

order: the judges who make fewer but more publicizable decisions in higher courts, or the magistrates and other members of the judiciary who make a far greater number of decisions, largely in courts of first instance rather than appellate courts, and whose decisions (it could be argued) may well be more cumulatively important even if not so widely publicized and quoted. The answer to this question is not self evident but a matter of judgement, and is taken up in the next subsection (subsection 4 below). R. F.

An interesting comment appears on pp. 198, 200 to the effect that the police and the machinery for maintaining public order are not considered by Hanson and Walles. In describing the institutions and patterns of interaction in the decision making process they have omitted the police, judiciary, and also the army – why? Does including them in the consideration prompt different conclusions about who are the decision makers?   D. J. M.

3.3   Block III – Agriculture

Apart from the analysis in Part 2 by Blunden and Jones, this block takes the position generally that to look for particular individuals or groups of individuals as 'making a decision' is not a very promising approach to the question of 'who?'; a case of misplaced concreteness. The approach in the set book and in the block generally is rather in terms of agricultural decisions

resulting from interactions between government authorities at various levels and the principal agricultural organizations which represent the industry. Evidence in the block shows pretty clearly that decisions, even quite practical decisions, are not made by one person or at one level but emanate from interlocking structures at various levels.

The question, 'who makes decisions?' could well be redefined in terms of 'who defines the goals of decision making in agriculture? and how do they define these goals?' The phrasing of the question in this form should help you in particular to focus on the extent

to which the National Farmers' Union define goals, and the extent to which this definition is influenced by the factors in the decision making process such as the role of the Cabinet, Parliament and the ministries.
                                    R. T.

However, Walters in Part 5 also refers to a 'leadership élite' in connection with specific agricultural decisions at the local levels. And there is suggestive comment by Potter in Part 6, 'Notes on an essay question', that as far as annual price review decisions are concerned, decision making appears to be 'increasingly concentrated in few hands'. Once again, then, one's answer to the

question of 'who?' depends to some extent on the way one looks at the evidence. If one looks at an annual price review or a local decision about rural housing, then one tends to find élites. If one looks at a whole set of specific decisions at different levels within a sector of decision making like agriculture, then one's answer will tend to be pluralist not élitist.

This comment appears to confuse the two separate approaches of identifying the decision making process, stressed at the beginning of the note on the agriculture block, and the alternative of starting from individual decisions which must be assessed first in terms of their importance.
                                    D. J. M.

Jones (Part 2) is somewhat singular in that he deals with the decision making behaviour of individuals. Some innovations, group buying for example, may require the co-operation of several farmers. Where this is not so the individual farmer's freedom to innovate will be circumscribed by his location relative to the centre of innovation, by group pressures, and by changes in his economic situation (perhaps brought about by changes in farming practice resulting

from the spread of innovations). Even so the propensity to innovate depends in part on the custom, character, and even caprice of individual farmers.

Some farmers are more important than others, however, and their attitude to an innovation may be decisive in its diffusion. Jones divides adopters into five categories of whom the first and last ('innovators' and 'laggards') are a 'deviant' minority while the majority occupy the middle part of his diffusion curve. He singles out a relatively small group of 'early adopters' as having the greatest opinion leadership of any adopted category in most communities. The existence of an opinion forming élite who condition the pace of change can be of critical importance in the decision making structure.
                                    A. B.

3.4   Block IV – Nationalized industries

In respect to this question, Block IV has adopted a rather different emphasis from other sectors by concentrating very closely on the central levels of decision making. Although considerations of planning, in Part 6, 'Decisions and impacts: a case study', and the preparation of the detailed proposals which a government department makes in relation to a particular industry in a given year suggest the continuous participation of many individuals in policy making (see comment by Brown in Reader about the point at which a decision can truly be said to have been formulated), the primary emphasis was on the major decision making role of the relevant Minister and Board Chairman (in particular, see Television Programme 8). It is an interesting speculation that the concentration of decision making uncovered by the course is a function, not of any intrinsic difference between sectors, but of the decision making level chosen by the different sectors. In other words, a study of the nationalized industries at area level might reveal the same access to decision making influence as that displayed in the Cheshire NFU. Comparably, a study of the health sector which focused largely on the relationship between the Ministry of Health and area hospital boards might reveal how restricted is access to major decision making. Note that if this speculation is true, it can either be a criticism or approval of the course structure depending on whether we have sufficient additional evidence to suggest whether there is some consistent relationship between participation in decision making and the level at which decisions are made.

In relation to this question there is a note about Block IV under models on pp. 59–60 that has a particular relevance.

D. J. M.

3.5   Block V – Health

Some important evidence is to be gleaned from Part 2, 'Regional disparities in the health sector'. Who are the people with the worst health, the poorest housing, the greatest unemployment, the smallest educational opportunity, and the lowest incomes? In what way are these characteristics correlated? On an *a priori* basis, one might imagine that such people were those who participated least in the making of decisions. Conversely, one might believe that those enjoying the best conditions were those individuals having the best access to the structure which fashioned those decisions. This would be an interesting question to investigate, although it is not pursued in this course.

In discussing regional disparities in the provision of health facilities one explanation which is offered is that practitioners often choose to work in the south-east or in hospitals which are medical teaching centres. This is an instance of a lot of in themselves minor decisions having a major impact. It raises the issue of the perceived area in which the authorities are free to make decisions. Obviously, the disparity could be ameliorated by some more or less overt direction of labour as would probably be practised in the Soviet block countries. In Britain, however, such a solution to regional disparities is not on the decision making agenda.

Is this in fact the situation? It might be worthwhile checking the accuracy of this observation against the section on general practitioners, and if there is a discrepancy considering the implications of this (Block V, Part 2, Subsection 16.1 and *Britain: an Official Handbook*, p. 137).   D. J. M.

Another sort of 'who?' question pertains to the level at which decisions are made. Here the whole question of the unification of the NHS structure raises issues about the degree to which local services catering to local needs should be responsive to local opinion and made by local decision makers elected through the democratic process.

There would seem to be some sort of apparent emphasis in the negotiated order model on the dispersal of decision making power. According to the model, everybody participates in decision making to some extent – even the patient, or the client of the authorities; even the prisoner detained at Her Majesty's Pleasure. Although it may be logically possible to combine this model with a belief in extreme disparities of decision making power, it is perhaps not

the emphasis one would expect (perhaps it could be done by suggesting that there were spheres of negotiation – prisoners are freer to negotiate on the quality of their food than the length of their incarceration?).

The material in the health block points up the contrast between different models of the decision making process. Willcocks, *The Creation of the National Health Service*, and Eckstein in the Reader stress the interaction between conflicting interest groups as they compete to influence the way authoritative decisions will be made; Kogan in Part 5, Section 1, abstracts the offices and roles established by the formal organization and ignores informal organizations, assuming that decision making is an activity of those with authority at the top; Strauss (in the Reader) and Roth (Part 5, Section 2) direct attention to the patients among others, and imply that no decision is a decision until it

is acted on and carried out, so that the whole process of perceiving, interpreting, applying (and negotiating and bargaining) is an integral part of the decision making process in society. Perhaps this suggests that it is not a matter of 'what level are you talking about?' but 'what is your conception of the decision making process?' Chasing after levels may be a misdirected activity; and your interpretation of the nature of the decision making process will determine in part your conclusion as to who are the decision makers. This point was explicitly introduced in Radio Programme 13.

D. J. M.

3.6 Block VI – Business

There is no clear cut answer given in Block VI to the question of who are the most important decision makers in the sphere of business, but a number of hints emerge about the main directions different writers have looked towards to answer this question. A number of authorities point toward *the controllers of big business* as at first sight anyway wielding the main power here: e.g. Miliband in the Reader, Finer as quoted in Grant and Marsh (Part 2 of the block) on the CBI as 'one of the most powerful and persistent of British pressure groups', and the constant representation of 'management' on the Economic Development Committees (discussed in Vaughan, Part 2) and similar bodies. On the other hand, a number of writers (e.g. Finer in the Reader, pp. 341 ff, and Grant and Marsh in Part 2 of the block) question whether there is conclusive evidence that those who control big capital are *in fact* the most important decision makers or are so in every respect, although it does at least seem to be assumed by most writers that their power is vastly greater than that of *small* businessmen (cf. Bolton's remarks in readings for Block VI on the ineffectiveness of small business as a pressure group).

The power of *government departments* in their various aspects comes out clearly in some of the materials. Nettl speaks of the focal part played by the higher civil servants (Reader, pp. 232 ff), Chapman illustrates the important part played by the Treasury in decision making (e.g. Chapman, 1969, p. 71) and Grove points out that

decisions about business are now taken less in Parliament as such than in Whitehall and various committees and commissions, etc. Thus it is now Whitehall and the members of commissions and committees that, significantly, form the main focus of pressure groups concerned with business (Reader, pp. 275, 279).

Less is said about the part played by *the trade unions* in decision making, but it emerges in several items that their power in this respect receives official recognition in their automatic representation on a number of crucial bodies (e.g. the Economic Development Committees discussed by Vaughan).

In fact, representation on official bodies (which, arguably, may constitute or include the most important decision makers) often seems to be seen as an attempted balance between representation of three main groupings: (1) management (presumably roughly equatable with the controllers of big business?) (2) unions (3) government departments. Grant and Marsh go so far as to state that 'the notion that the traditional constitutional trinity of King, Lords and Commons has been replaced by a new trinity of Whitehall, CBI and TUC has a certain credence . . .'. Even if this is acceptable, of course, further questions remain – like whether one can only look at this threefold power as a balance (if so, as a factual or an ideal one?) or whether one of the three groupings possesses clearly the most, or clearly the least, power of the three (and if so which?). At any rate, it is

51

interesting in this connection to note (as does Vaughan in the context of Economic Development Committees) that consumers as such are not normally represented, and are not mentioned as part of this new 'constitutional trinity'.

On the face of it, then, the main areas in which to look for the important decision makers are controllers of big business, government departments, and perhaps trade unions, with little potential power accorded to small businessmen or to consumers. However, there are hints that these latter two may assume greater importance at the *local* level (see Part 2 in the block, and Radio Programmes 26 (on the Warwick market) and 27 ('Small business and local government')). It is also arguable that perhaps small businessmen and (more emphatically) consumers may even make such a *number* of small decisions that (following the kind of analysis in Blocks II and V) they are *cumulatively* of the greatest importance as decision makers in the sphere of business.

A number of possible answers are thus indicated in the block (plus yet others which may emerge from the questionnaire project) and the choice among them is by no means foregone.   R. F.

3.7   Block VII – External relations

This block seems pretty explicit about an answer to the question of who makes the decisions. For example, the assertion is made by Vital, as cited in Barber, Part 3, Section 1, that 'the making of foreign policy . . . is the business of the executive and for almost all practical purposes the executive is unfettered in its exercise of this function'.

Likewise, and in elaboration of Vital's findings, Northedge concludes his lengthy analysis of 'Decision making in foreign policy' with the remark that the most important features in foreign policy making in Britain are: (a) the centralized character of British government in this field, (b) the prime importance of the Cabinet, the Foreign Office, the Treasury, the Defence and other Departments of State, and (c) the relative weakness of public opinion in this field. Foreign policy making is, as Barber points out, 'an élitist sport'.

At the same time, however, there is an effort to modify this élitist conclusion in Barber's paper on the national interest (Part 3, Section 1). The central proposition in his paper is announced as follows: 'decisions in foreign policy making are made in pursuit of the national interest which is identified, articulated and pursued by the government acting on behalf of the people'.

So the executive makes decisions on behalf of the people. But when the matter is directly confronted towards the end of the paper in 'In what sense can the government be said to act on behalf of the people?' an answer is not really attempted because of its great complexity and so on. For example, 'we shall not be able to develop the many facets of this question . . .' and 'we cannot enter into the debate about parliamentary democracy here, but we can note some of the particular characteristics that are found in foreign policy'. Among these characteristics is the point about the centralized, executive nature of decision making, and thus we are back again at the élitist conclusion found in the block. The definition of the national interest which appears to be most consistent with this conclusion is Paul Seabury's (cited on p. 42): the national interest is 'what the foreign policy makers say it is'.

The comments in the above note reflect very well the view that emerges from Block VII. What I think can be questioned (and this for me is a form of self questioning) is whether the élitist view of foreign policy making was not determined by the area which it was chosen closely to examine. The concentration in the block is upon the government of the state, and the officials who are charged with identifying and articulating the state's foreign policy. We might have reached very different conclusions if we had advanced an economic determinist view of foreign policy (i.e., that consciously or unconsciously decision making is shaped by economic development). In such a case we would have concentrated much more of our attention on industrial, financial, and agricultural decision making. A view could have emerged that the shaping of policy was largely dictated by a multitude of day to day decisions taken by business firms, banks, money houses, etc. A different élite, and even a pluralistic model of decision making might have emerged, and in such a context our concern with government would have been with the ministries most deeply involved in economic developments (a senior official of the Foreign Office told me in 1972 that the Foreign Office did not see trade or economic relations as one of its principal interests;

they were dealt with by other ministries).

Part 7, 'The multinational corporation' by Susan Strange (optional reading) makes an important contribution to this question of who makes the decisions by underlining the increasing importance of these corporations in influencing foreign policy decision making. The new view of decision making in foreign policy produces a new range of decision makers.   J. B.

3.8   Conclusion

In view of what the above notes tell us, the question of who makes decisions must boil down in the end to the annoying little phrase: it depends where you look. That is the principal conclusion to be drawn from the course regarding this question. As we think you'll agree with us, on reflection, this is a powerful kind of conclusion leading to a deeper understanding of the subject of decision making in Britain. An important lesson such understanding gives one is to beware of plunging behind those scenes over there to find individual decision makers before considering the assumptions underlying plunging in that particular direction, or of plunging at all.

Where one looks, and at what, is conditioned of course by the model or models one uses in analysis. The structure of this course has obliged us to look at decision making in sectors, that is, vertical slices of policy space in British society. This, in one sense, has been the model for this course. And what you must recognize is that this model has influenced any answer you have found to the question of who makes decisions in Britain.

For example, you cannot find either an élite or a ruling class in Britain in a course on decision making in Britain constructed as this one is. Thus, you may analyse decision X in the agriculture sector and find that it is made by élite A; decision Y in the sector on nationalized industry appears to be made by élite B; decision Z in the health sector seems to be made by élite C. There may be some overlap of élites, but the only conclusion you can come to, by virtue of the model used in the course as a whole, is that decision making in Britain is made by a plurality of competing and co-operating élites. And you know from your Reader that such phenomena are characterized ordinarily by social scientists as pluralism. The fact that nothing but a pluralistic answer is possible is a major difficulty with the approach adopted in this course. But it should be stressed that there are difficulties and limitations with alternative approaches to understanding the structure of power in British society.

Our own conclusions, based only on evidence provided in the course on public order, agriculture, nationalized industries, health and foreign policy, is that one tends to find a restricted number of people making important decisions at the national level. Decision making power at the local levels appears to be more widely dispersed. But that conclusion is governed by the evidence at our disposal in this course, and that evidence is there because the course model directed us to it. In other words, as we said before, any answer to the question of who are the most important decision makers in Britain depends on where you look for an answer.

A different conclusion on who the decision makers are is that it depends first on how you characterize the decision making process, and secondly on what you take as being important decisions (an issue pursued in the next subsection as well as in Part 1 of this block). Does the emphasis on levels represent a confusion between – or conflation of – the two approaches based first on process and secondly on what is an important decision? It is a given in this course that the course is concerned with the level (or arena) of the whole society – not with families, parishes or counties – and therefore a consideration of decision making at other levels or in other arenas must in some way be related back to the arena of the whole society.

If you confine your attention to the decision making process this course has provided a considerable body of empirical evidence and introduced a series of alternative models, and the application of these models in different sectors has brought out the significantly different conclusions that result as to who are the decision makers.

D. J. M.

The point above about the effect of the course structure on the kind of overall answer one tends to come out with is a valid one. Indeed it is one that it is essential to take account of if one is really taking a critical approach to sources (for the course material has to be treated as a source like any other). However, it could be disputed whether one should go quite so far as to say the course structure made an analysis in terms of an élite or ruling class *impossible*: myself I would say difficult, not impossible. Similarly I would argue that the pluralist answer is indeed made more plausible by the course structure, but query the statement that 'nothing but a pluralist answer is possible'. For one determined to find a different interpretation, there is plenty of material that could be tapped in the set books and elsewhere in the course (see also some essays in Part 2, Section 2). The final answer, therefore, remains in my view a matter for *interpretation* rather than a foregone conclusion.   R. F.

4   What are the important decisions?

4.1   Block I – Decision making in Britain: an introduction

Some major problems related to this question are laid out rather tersely by Potter in Part 2, Section 3, and are related both to the question of who makes the decisions and the question of what models are most useful for an understanding of decision making in Britain. Blocks II–VII need to be looked at in this regard and then the position summarized for the course as a whole. Nothing more need be said at this juncture.

4.2   Block II – Public order

The question of the importance of decisions is a problem which is treated in the block, but, perhaps, not satisfactorily resolved. One's reaction to the block as a whole was to be impressed by the evidence for the general diffusion of decision making, whilst simultaneously being convinced that a relatively small group have a crucial influence over the decisions that matter. It is important to realize that the two conclusion are not necessarily contradictory.

For an alternative assessment on this point see the note by R. F. on pp. 48–9 above.
                                        D. J. M.

The conclusion of 'Keeping the peace' in Part 5 raised the issue of the importance of decisions in a very clear form. If I was asked to assess the importance of the following as decision makers in the sphere of public order:
  (1)   Parliament
  (2)   Judiciary
  (3)   Police
  (4)   Public opinion
my answer would depend on what was the criterion of importance. If it was the number of decisions made (and a modified version of such a definition is implicit in the cited essay) my order of importance, given the evidence presented by the block, might be the reverse of the above. If, however, an important decision was one defined by the number of individuals affected by a given choice, my order of importance, based on the same evidence, might be as follows:
  (1)   Parliament
  (2)   House of Lords and appellate courts
  (3)   Chief constables and other very senior police officers
  (4)   Other judges
  (5)   Other policemen
  (6)   Public opinion
There is a useful point in the block about the possibility of small decisions being cumulatively equivalent to important decisions, particularly when they all tended in one main direction ('What Model?', Part 5, Section 4). This is something which needs taking up, and which may be illustrated elsewhere in the course. It is, perhaps, most important in the context of the example cited in the text, since if the Marxist model were correct, the tendency of lots of little decisions in one particular direction is just what one might expect (just as the independent decisions of multitudes of small capitalists leads to the eventual concentration of capital).

4.3   Block III – Agriculture

No attempt has been made in this block to classify the various types of decisions discussed as either important or unimportant. The eight contributors to the block, including Self and Storing in the set book, refer to some decisions as more important than others, in the usual way.

54

Perhaps in agriculture there have been no single decisions of great importance; even the passing of the 1947 Agricultural Act can probably be regarded as the outcome of a variety of small decisions.

You may find it useful again to rephrase the question.

Individual decisions may not be important but the goals which these decisions are designed to achieve are crucial. If so the important decisions are the ones which lead to the definition of goals.   R. T.

Beyond that, however, there are two separate distinctions between types of decisions which implicitly distinguish important from unimportant decisions. One is the distinction made in Part 2 by Jones and Blunden between long-term decisions involving planning or policy making (e.g. involving 'fundamental questions of choice, of enterprise, and allocation of capital resources'), and short-term organizational decisions ('made on a daily or weekly basis which may be based on the availability of workers, market conditions, or the weather'). The former are more important than the latter.

The other distinction is found in Walters (Part 5) where he distinguishes between national decisions which allow no room for local variation (e.g. a price review), and national or local decisions on which county or local organizations can exercise influence. Conventional usage would have it that the former are more important than the latter, although where Walters himself stands on this is unclear. Cheshire (Part 3) and Bowers (Part 4) more clearly accept Walters' distinction, where they identify as important those 'major policy shifts' from price supports to deficiency payments and now to tariff support, as well as the decisions embodied in the 1947 Agricultural Act; all these are national government decisions allowing of no local variation in their application.

4.4   Block IV – Nationalized industries

In a sense, the whole block is explicitly about important decisions. The criteria of importance are to be found in Wagner's introduction:

(a) The size of the nationalized industries (20 per cent of net capital, 30 per cent of new investment, etc).

(b) Impact on other industries.

(c) Use by the government as a means of controlling the economy.

On the whole, these criteria almost certainly bring most of the decisions discussed in the block into Potter's category of important decisions. (Note that the issue discussed above might in fact be rephrased so that participation in decision making was dependent, not on the level of decision making, but on the importance of the decisions being made.)

Part 2, 'The decision to nationalize', implicitly raises the question of whether there may not be another category of super-important decisions. A number of blocks deal with decision making areas whose major parameters were settled by decisions in the immediate post-war period. The decision to nationalize was one of these, to create a national health service was another, and the changes marked by the Agriculture Act of 1947 was another. In other words:

(a) Are there certain periods in which a whole series of fundamental decisions is taken?

(b) Is this period one of them? Many commentators have suggested that Heath's conservatism marks the end of the post-war settlement in British politics.

(c) What characterizes such fundamental decisions? Is it that they set the parameters of subsequent decision making?

4.5   Block V – Health

This block raised in acute form the question of whether the sector approach is one which can fully encompass the most important decisions and decision arenas. ('Decision arena' because very often it is not realized that decisions can be made. No one makes the decision that health facilities will be worse in the North and West; they fail to make, or fail to realize that they can make, decisions which will alleviate such a situation.) In raising the issues of how economic and social factors relate to the distribution of health and disease and the resources utilized to combat the latter it is pointing to decisions whose outcome affects the lives of all who live in Britain. However, these crucial parameters are subsequently taken as the framework in which decisions are made *within* the health service. Surely, though, the important questions about the health of the nation are those relating to the way in which the parameters are originally established:

(a) Why are the North and West so disadvantaged compared with the South and East?

(b) Why are medical services not allocated according to need?

(c) Why does the health sector receive the share of national resources it does?

(d) Why is the share of national resources devoted to health in Britain so much less than in other countries with a comparable standard of living?

Is it because an answer to any of these questions would take one far outside a sectoral approach that the course at no point attempts such questions?

In considering this point remember that there is much material in the required reading. Course texts do not duplicate what appears in the set books, and set books are a crucial part of the material on which this course is based. In the context of the National Health Service, Thomson, *England in the Twentieth Century*, Hanson and Walles, *Governing Britain*, Willcocks, *The Creation of the National Health Service* and Forsyth, *Doctors and State Medicine*, have a considerable importance.   D. J. M.

4.6   Block VII – External relations

The question is raised explicitly in the brief discussion of Holsti's notion of 'core' interests in the paper by Barber, Part 3, Section 1. This replaces, for Holsti, a concept of the national interest which he thinks is meaningless. A 'core' interest, like 'command of the seas', can change over time. Barber raises these questions: in the same way as asking who decides what are the important decisions, 'so we must ask: who says what are "core" interests?' Can we be sure that we can recognize them at the time, or is it only in retrospect that we can hope to distinguish them? If they are subject to change can they truly be described as 'core' interests? No answers are provided for these interesting questions.

Frankel in Part 3, Section 2, 'Britain's membership of the EEC and her national interest', opens with the statement that Britain's entry into the EEC is a 'major event in the evolution of British foreign policy'. An important decision is always a major event, but is a major event necessarily an important decision?

An aspect of decision making which is not mentioned in the notes, but which comes out strongly in examining the decision making process in the Foreign Office is the 'urgency' of some decisions. Matters often gain attention not necessarily because they are deemed 'important' but because they are 'urgent' – the business has to be done, the desk cleared, the letter answered, even if what the decision maker thinks is more 'important' has to be pushed aside.

In Block VII two decisions are examined in some depth – arms sales to South Africa, and British entry to the EEC. Why did I choose these decisions? Was it because I thought they were important? So far as I am able to make a self judgement I think the answer is because (a) I thought the entry to the EEC was 'very important' as it will mean a major reorientation of British foreign policy for the foreseeable future; (b) I thought the arms for South Africa question was less important (it does not impose a major reorientation) but was a good example of the process of decision making in foreign policy and the constraints involved. (I also chose it because I had previously undertaken research on South Africa's foreign policy and so it was an easy example for me to use. Was this the most 'important' reason for my choice?)
          J. B.

4.7   Conclusion

It seems fairly clear from our notes that this question falls on rather stony ground. The evidence provided in the sectors of the course does not appear to advance us clearly towards a consistent answer to the question: what are the important decisions in Britain?

The main reason for this is, of course, that there are no common criteria used throughout the course for identifying important decisions. In one sector the criteria for judging the question of importance are the number of decisions which can be cumulatively totalled on a single issue, and the number of persons affected by the choice. In another sector, it is suggested that the breaking point between important and unimportant decisions is the line between long-term and short-term consequences. In another block, size of arena seems the central criterion; national decisions are important because large numbers of people are affected. In another block, no criteria are to be found and the question itself seems hardly to arise at all.

To compound the confusion and extend the inconsistency of treatment on this question, there is the essay in Block I, Part 2, 'Decisions that matter'. The central criterion proposed there is degree of change of life style or world view by those affected by the decision. But that usage at the beginning of the course is not deployed in any subsequent block, as has been made clear in our notes for this question.

We appear to have arrived at the following rather bleak conclusion: that there is no answer to the question for the course as a whole in terms of the material provided in each of the sectors.

We believe, however, that it would be wrong to leave it at that. The point that needs to be underlined here is this: that explicitly to raise the question of importance at all is fairly novel in itself. Most social scientists simply assume implicitly that what they are writing about is important; for why else, they seem to say, should I bother to write about it? (They also assume that their students agree with them about what is important, a dubious assumption as you now know.)

What emerges from this course on decision making in Britain, in which the question of what is important is raised explicitly, is that the question is a difficult one and pursuing an answer to it leads quickly to fundamental issues in one's subject matter. One such fundamental issue that got raised in considering the question of what is important in this course was this: is one's unit of analysis – decision making in certain specified sectors – able to locate what is really fundamental to an understanding of the structure of power in British society? Just as this issue sprang from the question of what is important, so dealing effectively with it forces one back to the question of what is important. And on that question, you must in the end make a judgement. For a social scientist can as easily discuss, say, political power without making some judgements about what is and is not important as an art historian can discuss the history of art without making some judgements about what is and is not beautiful.

5   What models are most useful for an understanding of decision making in Britain?

5.1   Block I – Decision making in Britain: an introduction

The gist of the position taken in the block is that the concept of model is used in different ways by different people. No single usage for this course is laid down in Block I. The only thing to do in the circumstances as regards this question is to wait until the notes for Blocks II–VII are complete, and then take stock in relation to the question posed.

5.2   Block II – Public order

First of all we have a very clear outline of a model which, often in an implicit way, will be with us throughout the course. It will need to be stressed that this model can be used in conjunction with other models. In every single block an account of the formal structure could be given, and, at a minimum, it might be said that such an account gives us a framework within which our discussion can usefully proceed. This leads to an important question of whether more needs to be said for the model. *It is only when more is claimed that the sort of serious inadequacies arise that are mentioned in this block.* In fact, the issue arises of whether models can be asked to illuminate all of empirical reality, for, if they cannot, some doubt must arise about setting out to *disprove* the heuristic value of a model by showing what it does not explain. It may be that the only legitimate discussion of a model is to show those aspects of reality it does illuminate (since *a priori* it cannot illuminate the vast majority of aspects, which are necessarily better illuminated by other models).

In fact, I have a strong suspicion that this block and others have used the term 'model' in two rather different senses: as a complete picture of reality, which is more or less true, or as an heuristic tool illuminating certain areas of reality. These two usages would require altogether different evidence to establish their inadequacy:

(a)   In the first case, one would need to show that reality was substantially different from the model.

(b)   In the second case, one would need

to show that the promised illumination was, in fact, not forthcoming.

It appears to me that the case made by the block fits substantially into category (a), but that at times the conclusion seems to claim (b).

Another interesting point made about models is that different models themselves suggest that certain decisions are more important than others. This too involves a problem, since important here can refer to two separate qualities of decisions:

(a) Decisions may be important in some externally defined sense (that outlined in 'Decisions that matter' in Block I). Then the issue becomes one of whether a model offers illumina-

tion of decisions which fit that criterion of importance.

(b) Decisions may be crucial (important) to the degree that the way they are made offers evidence for a particular sort of model. Thus decisions taken according to a formal structural method are crucial for the formal structural model.

Obviously, another important characteristic of models that should be stressed is their interrelatedness. There are very close links between the model of informal, small, decisions and the 'negotiated order' discussed by Strauss *et al.* in the Reader, pp. 103–23.

5.3   Block III – Agriculture

In Part 2 Jones is described by Blunden as a 'model-builder if you like'. Blunden then goes on to say that Jones 'is attempting to postulate a common body of theory which explains in general terms the innovating propensity of farmers and the

process by which innovations are accepted or rejected by them over time and space'. Model and theory are interchangeable in this formulation. That's one way that the word 'model' is used in this block.

The word 'model' is not otherwise used very much in the agriculture block but it might be considered that the use of a model is implicit in the phrasing suggested on pp. 28 and 38. It is argued in effect that a proper model for understanding decision making in

agriculture is that the crucial factors are involved in the defining of goals and that the rest follows from the definition of goals and the way in which these are measured.

R. T.

The other way is to see a model as a tool of analysis within an approach to the building of successful theory. On this formulation, an approach to a field of investigation in social science includes basic purposes, definitions, models and assumptions. Criticisms of, or judgements about, each of these four aspects of an approach are made in terms of usefulness, not truth or falsity; and each of these aspects is useful to the extent that it contributes to the building of valid theory. Theory and approach in this formulation are distinct but also inseparable. A model, then: (a) is

a way of selecting and ordering facts such that the nature of the relationships between the facts are suggested; (b) cannot be falsified on grounds of evidence; (c) is one in a set of analytic tools with which the social scientist approaches a field of investigation. It is in terms of this latter formulation that élitist and pluralist models are introduced in this block. Questions are raised the answers to which can be approached in terms of one of several models. The student is required to select a model for purposes of analysis, or as an approach to a problem.

5.4   Block IV – Nationalized industries

Although analysis in terms of a goal seeking model has been restricted to Block IV, which has as its important characteristic the assumption that goals are set externally by the government (thus avoiding that fatal ambiguity involved in asking the question: But what are the goals?), it is important to note that each of the sectors discussed may be said to have goals. In the agriculture block this is explicitly mentioned in discussing the social goals which agricultural policy serves. In the other blocks, it

would not be too difficult to find statements which individuals involved in making decisions in the various sectors would agree to be their goals (thus a Chief Constable might say his goal was ensuring public order).

This latter raised what must be one of the chief problems of the goal seeking model – the degree to which goals are clearly and unequivocally identifiable. The police may argue that their goal is public order, while a Marxist critic of the police might suggest that the real goal was to act as a bastion against working class revolutionary activity. Who is right, in the absence of a charter of the institution (like the statutory provisions of the nationalized industries) setting out the goals for all to see? Moreover, this question also raises the issue of latent goals, which may be just as apparent in the nationalized industries as elsewhere (*viz* the footnoted comment that the Communists regard the nationalized industries as an instrument whereby the capitalists obtain cheap raw materials and power, p. 145, fn. 3).

Possibly, it could be argued that the goal seeking model has the vice which must necessarily correspond to its virtue. Its virtue is that it stresses the uniquely human ability to take actions (decisions) in the light of a consideration of their likely consequences. To say that someone has a goal is to say that he makes a decision between two or more alternative courses of action in the light of some criterion of choice; because he can consider likely consequences he can consider which alternative is most likely to contribute to some valued outcome. But while this is a crucial aspect of decision making, it is not always the only one or the most important one. As the material in the course and the Reader suggests, people often take decisions without anything like a full and rational consideration of the alternatives, or, perhaps, the situation is such that goals cannot be clearly formulated. Moreover, the consideration of consequences may be made in terms of an extremely limited goal (the intended impact) and our interest may be in all the other consequences which stem from a particular decision. Obviously, a lot of the devices discussed in the block (cost-benefit analysis, sophisticated definition of objectives) are all conscious attempts to make these problems manageable within the rubric of a goal seeking model. But even if this is possible where goals are as clearly delineated as in the nationalized industries, it must be much more questionable in other areas of decision making.

The previous notes referred to a 'fatal ambiguity' that can surround the issue of goals, especially goals of public policy. The ambiguity does not simply refer to the problematic identity of public policy objectives but to the fact that goals may be intermediate, just as ends may be means to some further ends. The problematic identity of objectives is illustrated on p. 39 by supposing that the British police believe their goal to be the maintenance of public order whereas a Communist would believe their goal to be preventive defence against the social revolution. The intermediate quality of goals may be illustrated by the argument that the establishment of a National Health Service is not for the simple purpose of improving people's health but for reducing absenteeism from employments and thereby accelerating the growth of economic production. There is also the uncertain measurability of public policy goals, especially in representative democracies, which inhibits a 'rational' pursuit of these objectives.

Given all these difficulties (which make any 'goal seeking model' of doubtful utility), there is some place for goal-orientated discussion in the decision making field. Governmentally we can discriminate two classes of issues: those which have, and those which have not, primary policy significance. In relation to the former and as preliminary to action on them, goal orientated discussion is unavoidable if the notion of policy is to retain some meaning. In relation to the latter, discussion would be irrelevant. Here we may take the case where in accordance with government policy the profitable sections of the nationalized Rolls Royce Company are being sold back to private enterprise: the correct decision about whom to sell to will emerge from officials following the 'proper' procedures and the 'proper' formalizing techniques. In the former class of case, however, a relevant example would be the originally proposed merger of British United Airlines, a private commercial enterprise, with BOAC, a public enterprise. The merger, which never came off but which the Minister was on the point of approving, collided with the interest of another private enterprise, Caledonian Airlines, in merging with BUA. Clearly, here was a policy problem, and such a problem always signals the need for a discussion about goals. For cases of such 'political' importance, no procedural specifications for decision making would be appropriate at any *sub-ministerial* level. But it is recognized, especially in the USA, that 'goal-orientated' preliminary discussion of this sort, though clearly called for in the name of public policy, is not what the situation always gets.

– Why?

This question is worth reflecting on.

J. M.

The main model stressed in this block is a goal seeking one. It needs therefore to be asked whether this is necessarily the only or most 'natural' model for analysing the nationalized industries. On the face of it – and in the light of the material presented in the block – the negotiated order model (to take just one example) might seem inappropriate. But if one brings into account facts like the effects on nationalized industries of industrial action in 1970–72 by workers in the railways or the electricity industry, or the result on the railways of 'working to the rules' rather than according to the usually accepted conventions (the negotiated order), is it then so self-evident that the negotiated order model is inappropriate?

Analogous points might also be made about other possible models here.

This brings one back to the point about models made in Block I (p. 124): that, in answering the question 'what models are most useful?', it is not simply a matter of examining the usefulness of a model for organizing the information already provided, but also of assessing its usefulness as a guide on what questions to ask and where to look.   R. F.

5.5   Block V – Health

The health block presents two models with almost diametrically opposed assumptions. In Part 5, Kogan's picture of the organizational structure suggests that the crucial variable in decision making situations is the nature of the authority roles. In contrast to situations where authority provides the key to decisions, the Strauss model in the Reader emphasizes that all decisions are a consequence of some sort of negotiation between the parties involved. This contrast shows us the truly complementary nature of models in the social sciences. Both sides provide sufficient evidence to show that their models are of some use in most situations. There can be few organizations which do not involve some degree of negotiation – a military organization might be an ideal type, but even a minimum of reflection on the interactions between officers and men offers evidence in favour of the interactionist thesis. Similarly, there are few organizations in which some element of authority is not present. *Once one is considering anything other than an ideal type both models can be simultaneously useful, even though the over-emphasis involved in the creation of a model leads to assumptions which appear to be contradictory.*

It may be arguable that the health sector is more suited to a negotiated order approach than many other sectors of the course. This is, in fact, demonstrated by Kogan who shows how the three separate organizational structures involved in the NHS and the complicated internal structure of the hospitals leads to the absence of cross-over points of authority. In areas in which authority is better defined, it is arguable that a negotiated order model would be less useful in illuminating the situation.

The contrast of models mentioned above raises a crucial problem for a decision making course (it could also be discussed under Question 1). The two models demonstrate the importance of negotiation and authority as determinants of decision

making behaviour. Most of the course is devoted to showing that determinants a, b, c, n^{-1} are related to the way decisions are made. However, except implicitly, and by putting a particular model at the forefront of the discussion, little attempt is made to *weigh* the relative importance of the various constraints which go to influence a given decision. In order to establish the importance of negotiation as compared with some other factor, one would need an empirical operationalization of the following kind (obviously, this argument applies *pari passu* to all the models and constraints mentioned in the course):

(a) One could measure the *potential area* in which decision makers were *free* to negotiate decisions.

(b) One could measure the *actual area* in which decision makers negotiated such decisions.

Only where both these variables were measurable could one assess the relative importance of negotiation in any particular case:

$$\frac{100}{1} \times \frac{\text{actual area}}{\text{potential area}} = \% \text{ negotiation}$$

of course, even 100% negotiation does not prove that the negotiated order approach is important. That depends on another relationship:

$$\frac{100}{1} \times \frac{\text{potential area of freedom to negotiate}}{\text{area in which there is no freedom to negotiate}}$$
$$= \% \text{ negotiated order}$$

It seems to me that anyone who wishes to say that negotiation is important in a particular case must establish a high value in the first equation. Anyone wishing to assert the relevance of the negotiated order approach (in preference to other modes of approach) must establish a high value in the second equation. N.B. Obviously, neither is possible in the mathematically exact form of an equation, but this form demonstrates what needs to be done.

Learmonth's essay in Part 2 on regional disparities in the health service anticipates but does not specify a *spatial model of decision making*. Such a model would require very clear definition of the variables which it considers. One of these is geographical space itself. To borrow an earlier phrase (Subsection 3, Conclusion) 'It depends where you look'. The essay and its tentative conclusions are dependent upon its initial division of England and Wales into two spatial units – the North and West and the South and East. Spatial scale may be defined, in part, by the nature of the problem or the data available. At the same time spatial scale may determine the data upon which observations are based and the significance of the problem itself.

It is pointed out that the broad regional contrasts conceal similarities that occur at smaller spatial scales. If different areal units were considered then a quite different pattern might emerge. This suggests a general question – should a variety of spatial scales be considered or should we seek to match particular problems to an appropriate scale?

This essay also reminds us that however objective our methods may appear the subjective selection of variables, data, and statistical techniques is inevitable. The analysis of a range of variables seems to suggest that there is a contrast between the morbidity and mortality experiences of the North and West as opposed to the South and East. This contrast does not appear to be reflected in a marked disparity in health service provision. What factors do account for the contrasts?

Of course, as Learmonth indicates, space is only one variable and not necessarily the most important. It may be that differences in health are better related to socio-economic characteristics than to geographical location. The two are often related, however. A consideration of all the variables is likely to yield the best explanation of a particular pattern.   A. B.

5.6   Block VI – Business

The notes above offer some criticisms of the goal seeking model. If such a model is not to be regarded as the most useful model for understanding decision making in Britain, what is?

If we were to look around for a model that seems both to have taken its rise *in reaction from* the goal seeking model and at the same time to have presented a way of decision making that (so it holds) not only reflects what usually happens in governmental and other choices but avoids the 'vices' of the model it reacts from, then this would have to be the incremental and mutual adjustment model that is briefly set out by Lindblom in the Reader extract (pp. 28–30). The extract begins by specifying the six features of the goal seeking model, the first of which is that decision makers face a given problem. But, according to Lindblom, 'Policy makers are not faced with a *given* problem. Instead they have to identify and formulate their problem . . . (and) there is all kinds of room for controversy over what "the problem" is. . . . Here already, then, is a limit on analytic policy making, and a necessary point of entry for "politics" and other "irrationalities" in policy making.'

At this point it is necessary to remark that, in Lindblom's view, the norms and underlying principles of the goal seeking model 'stem from criticisms of government decision making that take the form of observations that the process is not what one would suppose a rational process to be'. Next, we should make clear that the goal seeking model as well as Lindblom's own model are concerned primarily with co-operative and complex decision making, though Lindblom would claim that his own model is relevant also to such apparently trivial decisions as whether to marry, how many children to have, what occupation to follow, and so forth. On the basis of these preliminaries, Lindblom goes on to show that whether it is the choice of one's vocation or the fashioning of the nation's annual budget, the decisions 'are not so much comprehensively calculated as resolved through a limited evaluation' – sometimes taken as the mere by-products of other decisions (a decision does not necessarily imply an antecedent policy) and in any case (after all the factoring out of the decision making tasks) qualified by men's limited information and by their 'limited ability to grasp, calculate and remember.'

Because of these constraints, which even the advent of the computer has not eliminated, men's choices – according to Lindblom – are like the consumer's, i.e. only at the margin. As for choices within governmental decision making, Lindblom believes they are limited to the set of policy alternatives that are politically relevant. In a reasonably stable society like Britain, new policies would be only incrementally different from existing policies. Likewise in choosing between policy alternatives some of whose aspects offer, say, different increments of one or more values, Lindblom does not believe that our government would independently determine its objectives and then empirically analyse the consequences of policies for these objectives. It would intermix these value elements and these empirical elements in determining its choice, as we do when we go shopping.

This is by no means a full and adequate statement of the Lindblomian model. But it offers a brief elaboration of the Reader extract and suggests a few ideas to be taken into account in assessing the utility of those other models on which the course lays a greater stress. In particular, it might illuminate the manner in which small businessmen are accustomed to make their choices, even though it might say nothing directly about the major hypothesis of Block VI.   J. M.

The 'hypothesis' that is stated on p. 13 of this block is in at least some respects similar to some senses in which the word 'model' has been used in this course (see notes on 'model' in Block III above). Indeed a number of writers probably would, in certain contexts at least, refer to it as a 'model'. Certainly it shares the following characteristic with other models in the

course (e.g. the Marxist, or élitist, or pluralist models): that if one wishes to study the facts in the light of the model, or alternatively, look for evidence which relates to the model, one must analyse it into its constituent parts (some of which may be testable, some not). This process is discussed in Block VI (pp. 14 ff) and could in general also be applied to other models discussed in the course (e.g. if one wanted to make an investigation of the applicability of the pluralist model to Britain one would have to go through the same kind of process as part of and/or a preliminary to such investigation).

Thus, while no definite conclusion about the most useful model for understanding decision making in Britain can be stated on the basis of Block VI alone, it does emerge clearly that a final conclusion on this point needs to involve the same kind of analysis and operationalization of the various parts of the selected model(s) as is undertaken in Block VI.   R. F.

5.7   Block VII – External relations

It is not an explicit objective of the block to analyse on the basis of models. Also the concept of model is not used in this block. But there is a general 'picture' which is enunciated early in the block and integrates in a way what follows. This is found in Barber's proposition: 'decisions in foreign policy making are made in pursuit of the national interest which is identified, articulated and pursued by the government on behalf of the people.' This statement has the properties of a model and can be said to be useful as a tool of analysis. As a

'proposition', of course, it is neither confirmed nor falsified by evidence, although a lot of evidence in the block is related to this statement.

There is implicit in the block a set of assumptions which can be subsumed under a broad 'consensus orientation' to British politics and society in the material in the block. But I suppose this orientation is built right into the course itself, and is, therefore, unremarkable in this block. But it might be a point to develop in the synthesis part of this question.

5.8   Conclusion

As has already been stated, the introduction to models in Block I is content to introduce the different ways in which that term can be used. Furthermore the notes indicate clearly that terms like 'model' and 'approach' have been used somewhat differently in the course itself. This obviously creates enormous difficulties in providing a a straightforward answer to the question, for one has not merely to compare the usefulness of different models in looking at comparable material about decision making, but also to examine the extent to which the models outlined in the course are in themselves comparable instruments of analysis.

I think, however, that a common kernel of meaning can be isolated in the use of the term model, which does make the question a worthwhile one. This common meaning, or lowest common denominator of usage, suggests that a model (or approach)

provides us with a particular type of focus on the problem we are examining. A model offers this focus by delineating clearly the sort of answers which may be appropriate in a particular field of study without itself providing the answers. Thus, for example, Strauss's *negotiated order* model focuses on small scale interactions, and suggests that these are crucial for understanding decision making in health, without implying that we can understand *everything* about decision making in the health sector by utilizing this model. If the term 'model' has been used in this sort of way throughout the course – irrespective of what other meanings may at various points have overlain it – then a judgement in terms of usefulness is the only criterion of comparison that is viable in respect of models. They do not offer determinate answers, and so cannot be compared in terms of the validity of their findings. They only offer advice as to the type of answer one may find and their usefulness is a function of whether such answers can eventually be found.

This suggests a crucial point about models – that it is sensible to use many of them. Since models only offer useful illumination, and not truth, there is nothing to be lost, and much to be gained, by utilizing a range of models which can bring to light the many complementary facets of empirical reality. This should not be read to mean that all models are equally useful in all situations, for, as the preceding notes indicate, there are very good reasons to believe that certain types of models are ideally suited to particular areas of analysis.

Thus one might have a suspicion that a model which stresses the formal structure of government is more appropriate in analysing central government decision making, and a model which points to decisions made through small-scale interaction is more appropriate to decentralized decision making areas. What might appear to be the conclusion of our analysis is that the question can only really be answered by isolating the sort of areas in which the different models can be most illuminating. Once we know that, we will know the most useful sort of model to apply when we confront data which are new to us.

References

Britain: an Official Handbook (current ed.) London, HMSO.

CHAPMAN, R. A. (1969) *Decision Making*, London, Routledge and Kegan Paul.

HANSON, A. H. and WALLES, M. (1970) *Governing Britain*, London, Fontana.

THOMSON, D. (1965) *England in the Twentieth Century, 1914–1963*, Harmondsworth, Penguin.

WILLCOCKS, A. J. (1967) *The Creation of the National Health Service*, London, Routledge and Kegan Paul.

Section 2
Essays on selected topics

1   Are models useful?

By now, at the end of the course, two questions about models forcibly present themselves. (1) Why bother with models at all? (Why not, for example, dispense with them altogether, and instead go straight to the facts, or at least to testable theories and/or generalizations?) (2) If one *has* to introduce the term 'model', why not have one single definition and meaning instead of the present confusion?

What follows is a quick personal view on these two questions.

First, why have models anyway? This has been touched on in a number of places in the course[1] but, briefly, one central concern is to *abstract* from reality. We are faced with too many 'facts' or, at any rate, too many sources and are forced to some extent to simplify our analysis of them by abstracting certain of them as more relevant or significant than others. Again, we want to impose some sort of intellectual order on what might otherwise appear the chaos or confusion of the phenomena, and once more abstracting and focusing on certain aspects of reality by formulating them in terms of a 'model' is one way of doing this. Besides this, the element of intellectual enjoyment should be admitted too: it can be fun both formulating a model in verbal or visual terms and using it to abstract from and understand reality.

But more needs to be said than this. As far as the abstracting from and apprehending of reality goes, must *models* necessarily be involved? After all, abstraction is also a characteristic of, say, concepts, ideal types, generalizations – not to speak of the elusive but popular term 'theories'. One or both of two further characteristics are apparently also usually required for something to be a 'model'. First, a model, unlike a concept, involves some idea of complexity: there is a structure of internal relationships, not just a single part. A Marxist model, for instance, involves, among other things, positing both classes and the relations and dynamics between them. Secondly, a model involves an *imitation* of reality. In some sense at least there is correspondence (or a degree of isomorphism) between reality and the model, sometimes to the extent of being a one-to-one correspondence both between the parts of the model and the thing it represents and also (usually) between the dynamic relations of the model and the real thing. This characteristic has consequences for the further exploration of the model. Its correspondence to reality (its *isomorphism*) is a complex and a relative matter, one clearly highly relevant to how illuminating or otherwise the model proves to be, but not easy to fix definitively. Also, following from this, while one might ask about the degree of 'correspondence' to reality, one cannot ask about the truth or falsity *of the model itself*, for it is an imitation *of* reality not (as with, say, an empirically verifiable theory) a statement *about* reality.

The use of models in the rough sense just indicated would, then, briefly be to help us to apprehend reality, and the relation between different aspects of reality. Further, since everyone has certain sets of assumptions at the back of their minds in accordance with which they tend to structure their observation and analysis of reality, some of which at least they would not in the last resort

---

1   E.g. Block I, pp. 123–6; VIII, pp. 13 ff. esp. pp. 20–6, 31–2; IV, pp. 148 ff.

consider susceptible to disproof, it can be useful to be open about this by expressing them explicitly in the form of some specific model.

Why then – to turn to the second question – do people persist in employing this potentially useful term 'model' in such different senses? Some would omit the second characteristic above (complexity) and bring 'model' and 'concept' close in meaning, others would disregard the third characteristic (isomorphism), thus running together 'model' and at least some senses of that admittedly ambiguous word 'theory', or again 'model' and 'hypothesis'. These differences in usage persist widely in the social sciences. It is a matter for no surprise that, as has been pointed out several times (e.g. Block VIII pp. 21 and 57, Block I pp. 123–5), there are many instances of such differences in this course. At one point in the Reader, for example, 'concept' 'theory' and 'model' all occur within one paragraph, referring to more or less the same thing (Simon in Reader, p. 49), and at another 'theory', 'model' and 'explanatory device' are run closely together in a single paragraph (Scott in Reader, p. 21) with 'concept' used a little earlier again for much the same thing (ibid. p. 20). Again 'pluralism' is sometimes a 'model' (e.g. Block VIII p. 22, Reader, p. 288), sometimes a 'case' or 'rationale' (Presthus in Reader, pp. 331, 333) that could be 'demonstrated by . . . careful research' (ibid. p. 339), sometimes a 'theory' (Playford in Reader, p. 364). Similarly a Marxist analysis is sometimes a matter of 'fact' (e.g. Miliband in Reader, p. 303), sometimes a 'model' (see Block VIII, p. 22). Again, a model is sometimes 'derived from theoretical and logical foundations' and something against which social reality can be 'tested' (Jones on diffusion among farmers in Block III, p. 30); sometimes 'true' or otherwise (Block VIII, p. 57); sometimes something which could both 'simplify an otherwise intolerably complex situation' and also summarize 'conclusions about the nationalized industries' (Castles on the 'goal-seeking model', Block IV, pp. 149, 150); related to – or even identical with? – a 'hypothesis' (as in Block VI); or closely connected with the organizing concept of 'national interest' (Block VII). Other examples of differing usages in the course would not be far to seek.[1] It seems that these differences in usage are, for the moment at least, a fact of life in the social sciences that cannot just be wished away. Social science is not a tidy domain either in its concepts or its research findings. What is essential, however, is that such differences should be explicitly recognized.

There is a sense in which these differences are not *just* a matter of sloppy usage or of social science 'not yet having reached the stage' of agreed terminology or clear concepts. There would seem to be two other underlying reasons.

First, all of the three possible characteristics of models mentioned earlier are to some extent relative; one can have *degrees* of abstraction, of complexity and of isomorphism. That being so, what is to count as a 'model' is not a clear-cut and absolute matter but a matter of degree – and hence, inevitably, open to different emphases and interpretations. Thus, however rigorous one tries to be in the use of terms like 'theory', 'model', 'concept', there are bound to be areas in which they shade into each other. So, when certain things are isolated as 'models' in this course or elsewhere (e.g. the six 'models' discussed in Block VIII, pp. 22 ff), their 'model-ness' is relative rather than an immutable fact of life; they may well reappear in different guises in other contexts.

Secondly, since whichever of the three characteristics of a model we look at, the nature of its correspondence with 'the facts' is a complex and elusive one,[2] this means that statements about how far a particular model can or cannot be verified or falsified by the test of 'the facts' must themselves be correspondingly

---

1   For some other instances in Blocks II and III, see comments in Block VIII, pp. 57–63.

2   This is particularly so with the *isomorphic* characteristic, but applies to the other two also.

complex and elusive. It is therefore not surprising that people take up different, even internally inconsistent, positions on this. Apart from anything else, we do not have a situation in which some things are unanimously agreed as 'facts', other things as 'theories' or 'models'; if we did it might not be impossible to insist that some things are 'testable by the facts', others are not. But what counts as 'the facts' is partly a matter of interpretation: what a Marxist might call 'the facts' a pluralist might call 'a model', and vice versa. So even statements about the 'usefulness' of a model for viewing 'the facts', let alone questions of its correspondence to or isomorphism with reality, cannot hope to be self-evident or totally indisputable. Such points not only run us deep into problems in the philosophy of science but also remind us again of the significance of *interpretation*, whether we are talking of 'the facts', 'theories', 'models' or 'sources'.

In brief, I myself would conclude that 'model' is a useful term both for the reasons given earlier and because it is an additional reminder of the inescapable importance of *interpretation* in approaching the facts, and the way various *different* interpretations may be open to us. At the same time I would also suggest that 'model' is not a term that should normally be taken too solemnly or literally – for if one does, one runs up against these bafflements of its various different meanings and general elusiveness.

2   Decision making activity as pressure group politics

The substance of decision making activity in British politics can be subsumed in one phrase – pressure group politics. Discuss this contention in the light of the material contained in the D203 course.

This contention about the nature of group activity in the British decision making process suggests two rather different types of answer. First, it clearly implies that to understand the politics of decision making, one must understand the way pressure groups operate in a British context. The argument here is that groups play such a major role in the British political system that to study it in their absence would be rather like Hamlet without the Prince of Denmark. Secondly, the suggestion that pressure groups are at the centre of the decision making process can be taken to imply a particular theory about the locus of power in the arena of the whole society – a theory which in the context of this course has been described as pluralism.

That pressure groups are important in British society has been suggested at many points in this course. The operations of some of these have been described in some considerable detail in Blocks III and V, where the respective activities of the National Farmers' Union and the British Medical Association were outlined. In some ways, the most important lesson which emerges from the operation of both is the strategy they use to exert influence on the decision making process. In neither case do the groups make major efforts to convince public opinion (the one time the NFU tried it, it was a signal failure), but rather both typically operate by continuous contact with the civil service administration. That this is the favoured method of pressure utilized by established groups on the British scene is, of course, one of Eckstein's most important conclusions emerging from his study of the BMA, part of which is reprinted in the Reader.

Moreover, the examples of the NFU and BMA show clearly that pressure group activity is likely to be highly effective under certain circumstances. Certainly, the local branches of the NFU seem to have had a major impact in respect of those local issues with which they were concerned, and on the national scale the BMA and the other doctors' organizations were influential in shaping the form of the National Health Service. Nor does one have to rely on course material alone to see that pressure groups in Britain do have an important role in decision making. The newspapers are always full of one group making representations to government and Parliament on a particular topic and other groups making counter-representations. Furthermore, this process of representation is institutionalized in the British decision making system, and there are hundreds of advisory committees set up to advise and assist the government which have officially appointed group representatives.

It does seem then that it is fair comment to suggest the major role of group politics, and the impossibility of understanding the British decision making system without some reference to the phenomenon. However, as the concluding part of 'The doctors: interests in conflict' in Block V, Part 4, points out, a rightful emphasis on group politics can be carried too far if one fails to consider the constraints on their activity. Just as political parties are constrained by the views of their membership, and of the electorate expressed through the polls, so most British pressure groups are constrained by membership feeling, public opinion, and in particular the policies of the government in power, and what may be called 'the departmental view'. The constraining role of members' views is readily seen from the discussion in 'The doctors', which demonstrates that different attitudes, expressed in membership of different doctors' organizations, can have a major effect on the achievement of group goals. That the government is likely to be less than neutral in regard to some groups' proposals is testified to by the fact that the two most important sets of groups in the country – the employers and the trade unions – in their different ways support the two opposing parties.

That group activity is constrained perhaps already suggests some sort of minor caveat to the pluralist theory, which argues for the dominance of group competition as the means of making important decisions in society. Unless one is ready to call the government and the political parties groups (and some commentators have been – A. F. Bentley, for instance), then it must imply that to the extent that the government, the civil service departments, or the political parties, constrain group activity in general, it is not they alone which make the decisions. But the pluralist answer might be that in Britain *for the most part* it is the groups which constrain each other, and in the process of interaction the decisions are created which structure our political existence. There can be no question that to some extent this is a fair description. Groups do interact with each other and so create effects – one only has to consider the interaction of employers and trade unions and their joint effect on unemployment and inflation – and this is not merely peripheral, but plays a major role in British political life.

However, the pluralist case goes somewhat further than just implying that group interaction is a major factor in the creation of decisions and in forming the environment in which they are made by others. Pluralism is a prescriptive as well as a descriptive model, and it suggests that in some ways the groups which interact on the national scene balance each other and so create some sort of representation of views or interests. This is the aspect of the theory attacked by Playford in the Reader. He argues that there is absolutely no guarantee of balance, and that in any case the very concept of balance is dubious. Does it mean the views of one group weighed against those of another, or does it mean that group views should be weighted by their membership, or what? Furthermore, not all groups are represented in the so-called 'balance-of-power' system, and some therefore get no opportunity to express their views or interests. For this we have seen some evidence in Radio Programme 33, 'The Reformers', which demonstrates the difficulties under which reforming groups labour compared with the established interests in British society.

In summary, the *Decision making in Britain* course has demonstrated the crucial importance of group politics to understanding the reality of British politics, but it has not shown that it is the only key to understanding decision making, nor that a theory based on the dominance of group competition can fully encompass the realities of power in Britain.

3 The formal structure of government, constraints and hierarchy

In discussing what are the most important constraints on decision making in Britain, Castles argues in the note on p. 40 that in Block II the importance of the formal structure of government 'was dismissed with too little evidence'. My own view – and, from other notes by the same author, I suspect also his own view really – is that the importance of the constraints on governmental decision making exercised by the existence of the formal structure cannot be accurately assessed at the present time. The constraining effect, then, of the formal structure is not so much dismissed or denied in Block II as qualified by attention to other constraining factors, the relative importance of which, *vis-à-vis* the formal structure, cannot, in their turn, be accurately assessed. This seems to be implied by Castles on p. 38 where he observes, quite correctly, that the initial example given in Block I of a constraining factor, and the comments on this factor immediately offered, serve 'to announce a trend sustained through subsequent blocks of being satisfied to list different types of constraints . . . without . . . suggesting ways of measuring the degree of intensity of one constraint as opposed to another'. If this observation reads rather like a complaint, one has only to move ahead to subsequent notes to discover Castles' conclusion that 'the problem of weighting the factors or constraints remains' and that 'the impossibility' (in the author's opinion) 'of quantification in many social fields . . . means that the best one can hope for is a reasoned argument suggesting reasons for giving one factor more weight than another.'

The present essay aims to offer a reasoned argument, but the reasons it will offer are directed towards showing the complexity of any attempt to assign weights to the various constraining factors even in what Castles calls a merely 'linguistic 'way, e.g. 'A is more constraining than B'. The peculiar purpose of the essay, however, is to isolate a single constraint, *viz* the hierarchical arrangement of offices or officers involved in decision making processes of government, and to show that certain changes in the political culture over the last century and a half have modified drastically the traditional functioning of this organizational form, with probably long-term implications for how we assess, not so much the *importance* of the formal structure (this will be emphasized) as the direction of change in the relationship (never one of identity) between the way our political institutions work and the way we would suppose them to work from an examination of the formal structure itself.

It seems advisable first of all to clarify the meaning of what is meant by the government's 'formal structure'. In the present block, Murray has defined it as the institutions, procedures, and offices (functions and powers) that are established under the law and constitution. In Block II Murray has drawn attention to the three governmental branches – legislative, executive and judicial – which Montesquieu had characterized as the separated powers of every constitutional government. In the same block, however, Palley and Power make perfectly clear that law-making is not confined to the legislative branch, nor adjudication to the judicial branch, any more than administration is confined to the executive branch. This mixture of powers within each branch is a characteristic feature of decision making in such a government as our own. Also characteristic is the mixture of formal and informal elements within the decision making process. It is true that what emanates from the organs of government as statute law (i.e. primary law) or as executive routine or (when lawfully exercised) as administrative discretion is a product of the formal structure. But this fails to express all that happens in and through the processes of government. To take only a single example, Palley (Block II, p. 45) is concerned to stress the extra-constitutional factors that bear on the decisions of judges and also the uncertainties 'as to which of the many rules of the law is applicable' to this or that situation and even 'as to the scope of the rules'. All of which goes to show that government involves interactions that are highly complex and may be quite ambiguous in their significance. This is not to suggest that the formal structure of government is hardly important. On the contrary, its importance can be immediately discerned if we suppose that this formal structure is somehow abolished 'at a stroke' and realistically assess the consequence. Certainly, we cannot realistically conceive that, except by temporary operation of the law of inertia, everything will go on as before in the total absence of the formal structure.

The argument so far has had two closely related purposes – first to discuss how informal factors modify the functioning of the formal structure, though without eliminating its importance; second, to show that within each major branch of government one kind of power is interacting with and being modified by other kinds of power, just as modifications occur through the interactions of the three branches of government *inter se*. The conclusion seems inescapable that the British government today is a system that operates by built-in constraints – the informal constraining the formal and *vice versa*, and the executive, legislative and judicial powers constraining each other both within and between the major governmental branches. It is time now to examine how the constraining factor of hierarchy in government organization actually functions and what changes may be discerned in this mode of functioning when we extend our time-scale to cover the nineteenth as well as the twentieth century. Hierarchy is a vertical arrangement of institutions and offices. We see it in the relations of the Houses of Parliament, in the whole system of courts and, most impressively, in the bureaucracy. There are relations of superordination and subordination. These relations are implied on p. 42 which says *à propos* of the nationalized industries that 'constraints can be deliberately constructed as a means by which one decision maker sets the operating parameters for a lower level decision maker in government'. The same relations are being referred to when Barber in his notes to Radio Programme 6 asks students to try to identify, in connection with order in the streets, which decisions are taken and what discretion is exercised by particular policemen occupying different points in a hierarchy.

Each of the last two references implies a view of hierarchy as an organizational form (part of the formal structure of government) which emphasizes the responsibility of subordinates to their superiors. 'Power directs everything, surveys everything' and the officers of executive power 'are, each in the portion of authority confided to it, authority in action'. Hierarchy as a principle built into early modern bureaucracy supported what Weber called 'monocratic authority', ensuring centralization, discipline, obedience. But, as David Hume somewhere said, we do not necessarily understand a thing correctly in terms of its origin. Since the early modern age, hierarchy has had to function within more complex social contexts – notably within representative, political democracies. Its 'spirit' may be favourable to authoritarian centralism, but this is not necessarily the way it works. The Reform Act which modestly extended the franchise in 1832 was followed within four years by the remark of Sir Henry Taylor in *The Statesman* that 'the execution of the laws deals with those particulars by an induction of which the results to be aimed at in legislation are to be ascertained, and the generalization from those particulars can only be well effected when the lowest in the chain of functionaries is made subsidiary to the

operations of the highest in a suggestive as well as in an executive capacity. . . .'
This attempted change in the functioning of hierarchy was small-scale and
perhaps reluctant, but it did point to a new situation where, with universal
franchise, public servants at every level were to be related in some positive way
to the democratic political process and where collegiality as distinct from
esprit de corps could establish itself in the public service. By 1956 Lord Strang,
a former Permanent Under-Secretary of State for Foreign Affairs, could insist
in his *Home and Abroad* that even the disciplining of 'juniors' must be 'couched
in terms proper *from one colleague to another, both engaged in the same enterprise*'.
These words of a British administrator carry almost the flavour of H. A.
Simon's dictum, that 'When two men co-operate to roll a stone that neither
could have rolled alone, the rudiments of administration have appeared'.
True, the principle of hierarchy has been carried over from the structure of
monocratic authority to the context of ministerial responsibility in government,
but the shift towards thinking of government as *co-operative activity*, as a planning
and carrying out of purposes agreed to, with whatever mutual accommodations
both within and outside of the formal structure, carries a hint that, in the
authority structure, the continuing relationships of superordination and
subordination are, in the last analysis, less important than the equality of
persons in these relationships.

Hints, unfortunately, are not quantifiable. We simply do not know the
relative weight of constraints in a system of government where, at every level,
'argument has an office' (to use Bagehot's phrase), where the increasing
importance of technical and scientific knowledge for the effective transaction
of public affairs renders increasingly irrelevant and potentially obstructive
some of the differentiation of staff levels which personnel classification agencies
have developed over the years, and where with power so divided that each
power element is compelled to interact with the others, no institution can be
undeniably sovereign. The processes of constraint are upwards and downwards,
and the bearers of these constraints are ceaselessly bringing together the
elements of decisions. In these circumstances, we would be hard put to it to
come down in favour of any firm and precise conclusion about how power is
distributed and operates in our society. But we do know the direction of change
and that it is one which constantly blurs the picture of the formal governmental
structure as an adequate representation of the true state of affairs.

4   Is an élitist interpretation of the decision making course possible?

'Among the constant facts and tendencies that are to be found in all political
organisms, one is so obvious that it is apparent to the most casual eye. In all
societies two classes of people appear – a class that rules and a class that is
ruled.'[1]

The central core of élitist theory is the belief in the inevitability of an élite/
mass dichotomy. This dichotomy has been explained in many different ways.
For some (Mosca, Michels) the explanation lay primarily in the peculiar
constraints imposed by the difficulties of organization. For others, notably
Pareto, this division was the natural result of human attributes constant
throughout history. James Burnham, who attempted to synthesize classical
élitism with Marxism, believed that an élite was a continuous feature of society
because of the skills necessary to control economic production. Wright Mills
developed from this the thesis that certain key institutions in society are always

---

1   Mosca (1939), p. 50.

controlled and dominated by a few men, who perpetuate their own position of power.[1]

Thus, while a central core exists which enables us to talk about a body of élitist theory, it is by no means a simple task to apply these generalized and diverse explanations to the specific empirical data produced in a course like *Decision making in Britain*. This is particularly true since it is not the simple assertion of a dichotomy between élite and ruled but the assertion of its inevitability which is distinctive about élitist theory and it is in an explanation of this point that the élitists differ.

This situation is further complicated by the fact that the classical élitist theory of the late nineteenth and early twentieth century was formulated as part of a rebuttal of the two most important rival theories of the time – namely the theory of representative democracy on the one hand and Marxism on the other.[2] Neither of these theories have been considered central to the decision making course, with the result that the evidence which the élitists saw as crucial is omitted.

However, a few points can be made here. Firstly, classical élite theorists, in contrast to the nineteenth century belief that the formal structure of the political process and the democratic ideology which encapsulated it disclosed the reality of power and decision making in democratic systems, suggested that such formal institutions were a façade which obscured the reality of élite rule. Much of the evidence produced in the course (notably in the Public Order block sections on the judges, the Health block sections on negotiations with doctors, and the Agriculture block sections on NFU negotiations) has tended to support the view that the actual character of decision making in British society and the power relations that this discloses cannot be very accurately discerned from a simple consideration of the formal structure of the decision making process. In more specific terms a study of the parliamentary process,[3] nominally supreme in decision making, tells us very little about the patterns of executive decisions taken in the context of characteristically confidential negotiations with a multiplicity of pressure groups who are in no sense representative of the interests of the electorate as a whole. Now while many writers have argued that 'pressure group politics' enhance rather than detract from the democratic process, it is also possible to take the view that they represent 'sinister interests' operating against the interests of democracy; this is certainly the view that Pareto and Mosca would have taken, with the proviso that, however operated, democracy would always breed such 'sinister interests'. (For a further discussion of the relationship between the theory of democracy and pressure groups, see Reader, pp. 331–9 and 389–407.) To take another theme which has recurred throughout our case studies, the idea that the formal ideological legitimation of patterns of decision making may serve to obscure the motives and influences at work on the decision making process (cf. especially the Public Order block) would be one that is quite at home within the structure of élite theory.

A further strand in classical élitist theory was the rejection of the view that the mass electorate took an active and well informed interest in the conduct of politics and was thus both qualified and able to determine the frame of reference within which their representatives took decisions on their behalf.

1   The key texts for élitist theory are Pareto (1935), Mosca (1939), Michels (1958), Burnham (1942) and Wright Mills (1956). For a clear and useful summary of their work, see Parry (1969).

2   In a rather different context, this is equally true of the élitist theorists of the 1940s and 1950s, Burnham and Wright Mills.

3   See also Hanson and Walles (1970), pp. 62–3, for a discussion of the very select nature of parliamentary representation and the Reader, pp. 293–303, for a discussion of the way in which different groups with direct access to government are dominated by a select few.

The élitists posed against this the idea that the mass was both manipulated by the élite and capable of manipulation because of its apathy and irrationality. The course has not considered in any depth those people who are not organized in society, but has, perhaps significantly, concentrated either on the power-holders in society – the judges, the police, the heads of the nationalized industries, the doctors – or on those who have actually participated in the decision making process (sometimes unsuccessfully, like the agricultural workers). The exception to this is the consideration of the power of patients in the concept of the negotiated order in the Health block. This exception is interesting because it concentrates only on small-group interaction, and the difficulty of applying this concept to larger organizations or of assessing the extent to which patients exercise power might suggest that Michels was correct in assuming that an élite was inevitable in complex organizations, and that the analysis in fact conceals a power structure present even in small organizations.

It might well be thought that, in one respect at least, the findings of the course run decisively counter to the assertions of élite theorists. While it may well be true, as the élitists would accept, that power, and hence the ability to influence decisions, is not evenly distributed throughout society as a whole, the analysis of the role of pressure groups, etc., in the Health, Agriculture, and External Relations blocks does appear to point to a pattern of dispersal of power, albeit an unequal dispersal, which runs counter to the élitist conception of a concentration of effective power within a small élite. This refutation is itself based upon a misapprehension as to the assertions of élite theory, which while asserting that there is a concentration of power vertically in society, as between the élite and the mass, does not rule out a certain dispersal of power horizontally in society, as between say the political élite and economic or other élites. Moreover, the degree of homogeneity within any one élite group is historically a variable in their view. It would thus be open for adherents of an élite theory to argue that what is characteristically described as 'pressure group politics' is no more than the form which relations between different élites, or for that matter, between different sections of the same élite, usually take in advanced industrial societies. Certainly, the emphasis placed by pressure group theorists on the basic consensus underlying all the participants in the process, and their concern for incremental change, would tend to reinforce such an élitist perspective.

Very little more can be said about the applicability of élite theory to the course. In particular, no evidence can be conclusively provided as to the nature of the ruling élite. While the particular illustrative themes considered show some positive connection between the perspectives of élite theory and the findings of the course, or, put more negatively, those findings do not provide us with any firm grounds for a decisive rejection of élite theory, at the same time the evidence provided could equally well be explained by reference to Marxist theory, with which it has a few similarities. The basic difference between the two theories – one which however hard Burnham may have tried makes them impossible to synthesize – lies in the *explanation* of the power base of the ruling class or ruling élite. For Marx, the existence of a ruling class was a consequence of the contingent fact of class societies; a proletarian revolution which abolished capitalism would abolish all class rule and substitute in its place a true socialist democracy. For Pareto and Mosca on the other hand, élite rule was a necessary constituent of all societies, and a so-called 'proletarian revolution' would simply result in the replacement of one type of élite by another. The essential problem for our purposes here is that while one can produce evidence for both theories which point to the existence of a ruling class or ruling élite, there must be some explanation of how this stratification has come about in order to choose between the two theories. In general, since the course has not been wedded to explaining or expanding either of these two theories, the evidence which would enable us to make a judgement either way is simply not present.

5   Is a Marxist analysis possible?[1]

The implications of adopting a 'Marxist' analysis are of course more complex than can be covered in this short essay, but briefly the two central tenets are: (1) the central importance of the existence of several social classes in society, principally the ruling class (i.e. the bourgeoisie in modern capitalist society) as opposed to the proletariat or workers; and (2) the crucial significance of the economic element in society, both in differentiating the classes (according, that is, to their respective relationship to the economic mode of production) and as constituting the basic underlying structure in any society.

This type of interpretation is often by-passed and ignored in social science analyses of contemporary Britain. In this course, for instance, the division of the material in terms of actual sectors of government according to the assumptions of a formal structural model means that questions about the power of a certain class right across society do not raise themselves explicitly and are not so easy to treat. But this (and other) models are not pursued comprehensively throughout the course, and in any case evidence that leads to a Marxist interpretation of the facts of British society cannot be wholly concealed even by the use of superficially quite contradictory models. Even on the basis of the material before us, then,[2] it is possible to sketch out a Marxist analysis of decision making in Britain.

Thus, even if one begins from a formal structural model as a clue to identifying the locus of power in Britain (a common approach in this course), it is clear that it is the ruling class not the proletariat that holds the reins of this power in whatever sector we consider. At the head is always the representative of the hereditary ruling family (*Britain: an Official Handbook*, pp. 26 ff), with its background of hereditary wealth. Then there is Parliament. This comprises, first, the House of Lords whose members 'are not responsible to any electorate and the bulk of their number sit by virtue of birth' (Hanson and Walles, 1970, p. 85. On figures showing the balance of hereditary as against non-hereditary members, see *ibid.*, p. 85, n. 32). Second comes the House of Commons which *appears* to represent the people. But the nature of this representation needs to be seen against the actual make-up of the membership, which is heavily weighted in both the major parties towards managerial and professional interests with little to no real representation of the workers, particularly in the Conservative Party. (For some figures see Hanson and Walles, 1970, pp. 62–3.) Furthermore, by their opposition to proportional representation and other devices, the two parties join in retaining the reins of power in their hands, and give no opportunity for newer or truly proletarian parties to win power. The working class, given no other choice, continues its habitual support of the two established parties (see Hanson and Walles, 1970, p. 32). So, even starting

---

1   I am not myself necessarily convinced of the validity in all respects of such an analysis (and certainly would not hold that it is the *only* possible one) but since I think a strong case can be made out for the possibility of a Marxist analysis I have provided the following sketch. Obviously only brief indications of the sorts of interpretations possible can be given within the compass of a brief essay. For some further points see also discussions by Miliband and by Baran and Sweezy in Reader (pp. 293 ff., 304 ff.) and Radio Programme 32, 'The revolutionaries'. For a critique of a Marxist analysis as applied to Britain, see the extract from Crosland's well-known work in Reader (pp. 317 ff.), also certain points in Nettl in Reader (pp. 232 ff.).

2   I.e. in correspondence and broadcast material, set books and recommended reading. (Apart from one quotation from Marx only evidence from these sources is used in this essay: some you may well wish to interpret in a different way.)

from a formal structural model about where to locate central decision making, the facts inevitably push us towards accepting that power is held by a ruling class, with the proletariat excluded from any real access to that power.

One can reinforce this by looking at the two other wings of government in the formal model. First the judiciary. Here it has been stated that 'the background of the English judiciary is largely upper middle class, and most judges have been educated at public schools' (Block II, p. 92; cf. also p. 93 and pp. 117–21). Admittedly not all members of the judiciary are judges, but even at the other end of the scale the lay magistrates are selected from 'prominent members of the community' (Block II, p. 122) and it is likely that class bias enters in here too. With the civil service, on the other hand, recruitment is on a different basis and apparently more open (though Oxford and Cambridge still form the main source of 'open competition' recruits (Hanson and Walles, 1970, p. 137). But the ethos of Whitehall is something into which recruits tend to get socialized whatever their original connections with the workers: 'like a magnet, it sucks in members . . . [and] emasculates [other] groups, while preserving their outward shell of autonomy and independence' (Nettl in Reader, p. 232). In such ways, the ruling class preserves and reinforces its power, despite the façade of autonomous or disinterested decision making within government.

If one moves away from the formal model this analysis becomes even more convincing, for one can discern the economic structuring behind all this. There are the close relations between business and government: access of big businessmen to government and Whitehall circles (see cautious remarks by Finer on this, also Nettl, in Reader, pp. 340 ff and 249); contacts between the Treasury and the Bank of England (Chapman, 1969); potential connections between senior civil servants and boards of private companies (Grove in Reader, p. 281); the 'daily contact' between the capitalist CBI and the government, involving 'continuous exchange of views' (Block VI, Part 2, p. 66); and the business connections and background of many members of the government (see Miliband in Reader, p. 302; Hanson and Walles, 1970, p. 63 on company directors among Conservative parliamentary candidates). It is no surprise that the distribution of wealth in Britain apparently runs parallel to this. Thus personal income from property (rent, dividends and interest) made up 11 per cent of total personal income in 1970 (*Britain: an Official Handbook*, p. 199) and this 'adds to the income of the already affluent' (*loc. cit.*) as distinct from the majority – the wage-earning proletariat.

It may be true, as Crosland points out (Reader, p. 319), that a certain amount of economic power has now passed from the capitalist class to government control. But against this one can argue that the stock case of this always cited – the nationalized industries – make up only one minority part of industry: in 1967 for instance they employed only 7 per cent of the total working population (see figures in Reid and Allen, 1970, pp. 14–16), and it is still true that 'most manufacturing is in the hands of private enterprise' (*Britain: an Official Handbook*, p. 200). Furthermore when *control* even in the nationalized industries – let alone the private sector – is not in fact in the hands of the workers, there is no real 'public' ownership in the sense of power by the proletariat. Control of decisions even in the 'public enterprises' remains firmly in the hands of the top managers and the government (see Block IV) – in other words of the ruling class. The decision making process furthermore continues to go on behind the scenes through 'informal contacts' and 'a system of influence which evades scrutiny' (Block VI, Part 2, p. 59). As it is summed up in one recent Marxist analysis, 'Most of the country's wealth is owned by a very small part of the population. This minority also controls industry and wields the main economic and political power' (H. Frankel, quoted in Block I, p. 152).

The whole system, furthermore, works to the benefit of the rulers. The 'national interest' is invoked as a smoke screen to blind the proletariat to the capitalist interests at work behind decisions about selling arms to South Africa or expanding markets in the EEC (Block VII); and business organizations – the forces of international capitalism – continue to exert their hidden influences on and behind governments (Block VII) and to squeeze out the small trader who falls and becomes submerged in the proletariat (one possible interpretation in Block VI). Nationalized industries are controlled from the top, not by the workers, and this means that its goals are ultimately decided by the ruling class (Block IV). Organized labour may have had a brief success in stopping the rulers' attempt to fetter the working class by its Industrial Relations Bill (Television Programme 1, on the Labour decision to withdraw their Industrial Relations Bill), but the forces of organized capital were to prevail in the end (see Radio Programme 4, on the Conservative implementation of this bill). The landowners[1] have their position bolstered by the system of agricultural subsidies to farmers (Block III, e.g. Dossier, p. 13, item 3) – while the struggling workers on these farms are kept in their place by receiving one of the lowest wages in the economy (Block III, Dossier, p. 31).

Perhaps of even more interest is the insidious way in which the ruling class allows the proletariat the illusion of freedom to make decisions while at the same time ensuring either that these decisions involve no real choice or that the end result is to the rulers' interests. It is all very well to write about the way decisions are diffused or about people's perceptions and negotiations (as in, for example, Blocks II and V). But whence are these perceptions and decisions derived? And whom do they ultimately benefit? In Britain too 'the class which has the means of material production at its disposal, has control at the same time over the means of mental production. . . . They . . . rule also as thinkers, as producers of ideas, and regulate the production and distribution of the ideas of their age' (Marx, *German Ideology*). For example, we can speak of the decision making process diffused throughout society as individual policemen and members of the public interact, negotiate and decide in the sphere of public order (Block II) – but in what direction do all the decisions seem to tend? Apparently to a view of crime as expected of (and imposed on) the working class – a self-reinforcing idea that in turn reinforces the power of the ruling class against the workers. And this is without the participants ever being aware of the forces which condition the part they play! Again, the many small decisions by outwardly free agents like farmers or shop-keepers (Blocks III and VI) can have vast and continuing implications for the structure of society – and yet the agents may have no inkling of the economic structure which conditions their choices in certain directions. Again, the way in which the mass media can edit the material that they propagate – indeed, as Television Programme 2 demonstrates, inevitably *must* so edit it – gives the rulers yet further insidious ways of indirectly controlling the ideas communicated to the proletariat. Further, the real state of affairs is effectively concealed by the way television inevitably plays up the personalized model and minimizes economic forces (see Television Programme 2) and by the stress on interviews in the mass media – a form in which the economic and class forces which, unaware, structure the people's choices can seldom be elucidated (see Radio Programme 9). The real determining forces are thus kept effectively hidden from the workers.

So even the parts in this course which stress the opportunity for the people to make decisions and the meanings they attach to these provide evidence not

---

1 In Marxist writings sometimes distinguished as a separate class, sometimes incorporated into the ruling class.

against, but *for* a Marxist interpretation. For while the proletariat can be deceived into believing itself free and remain unaware that its very ideas are controlled by the economic structure of society to the benefit of the ruling class, so long can the ruling class retain its hold not only on the organs of economic and political power but also on the mental production and decision making processes in the society.

6   Does television favour the 'great man' theory of decision making?

It is a commonplace that the use of any medium of communication involves the selection of material. The question here is whether television has in-built characteristics which systematically favour the choice of material supporting a particular interpretation of social events (the 'great man' theory). My argument will be that no medium embodies *intrinsic* characteristics as broad and unchanging as the question implies. If TV programmes display a predisposition towards any one theory of decision making, we must seek explanations in the wider processes of society. But, in rejecting notions about inherent properties, we are obliged to offer an alternative perspective which will elucidate those broad but *variable* characteristics which television manifests in a given society. However, we will dispute the hypothesis that even these features can 'favour'[1] any theoretical orientation (though not necessarily denying that some orientations appear more frequently than others). Again, explanations must be sought elsewhere.

In Television Programme 2 Stuart Hall suggested that television *as a medium* possesses characteristics which make it easier to document a decision in terms of the influence of the central actors (the 'great men') than in terms of the other four theories of decision making proposed in Block I. In his delineation of the medium he cites factors like the limitation on finance and production time, the impact of visual material, the well-established routines of presentation, and the notions of producers and presenters as to what is important about an event. But only the second of these could seriously be held to constitute an inherent property of television: the remainder are *features of a medium within a particular social structure*. The latter, by determining the medium's functions, helps to condition its character.

A generally valid definition of 'television' must therefore restrict its reference to only the most fundamental physical characteristics. In essence television comprises a camera, a means of transmission, a television receiver – and, of course, people to send and receive 'messages'. It can be used to carry pictures and sound from a hospital operating theatre to another room for the benefit of half a dozen medical students, it can be used by store detectives for the scrutiny of every counter in a supermarket, or it can be used to transmit an acted drama from a highly sophisticated television studio to an audience of millions. In each case function is decisive. We should be surprised if the closed-circuit television coverage of a four-hour surgical operation displayed the sort of drastic editorializing described by Stuart Hall, and we would not expect a supermarket observation system to incline towards a 'great man' narrative. And if programmes on the national TV networks are affected by financial considerations, this is partly because society distributes priorities in a certain way.[2] In fact Stuart Hall sometimes highlights the social origins of elements of

---

1   In the sense of '*encouraging* the selection of material' as distinct from *permitting* it.

2   With existing technology it would be possible to provide a home audience with a wide choice of national and local television channels. However, large sums of money would be required to lay a cable network.

the medium. My point is that, unless we succeed in further clarifying the relationship between social forms and such attributes as media reveal in any given context, we may actually be discouraged from seeking more adequate explanations of media phenomena than 'intrinsic characteristics' analyses will permit. In short, the first three words of the question disclose an implicit conception of 'television' which is of dubious value.

Yet, given that the applications of the medium – and therefore its complexion – are institutionalized, one more question remains to be answered: does television, *as constituted in our society*, lend itself particularly to 'great man' interpretations? Stuart Hall's argument here seems to pursue two principal lines; firstly that the limitation on resources encourages producers to collect material most conveniently to hand, and secondly that pressures to condense their arguments attract them to subject matter with sharp impact. There is a consequent temptation to narrate any series of events in terms of 'witnessed accounts' (interviews), ensuring that the resulting programme will be 'short on background'. The influences of economic factors and historical traditions are difficult to capture, while the vivid individual reports focus attention on day-to-day decision making – the 'foreground'.

It is difficult to understand why 'personalized' accounts *need* be of this nature; it would seem rather to depend on how they are used and what significance they are accorded within the structure of the programme. After all, economic forces and historical traditions express themselves partly through the conscious intentions and attitudes of social groups, and individual informants can be chosen to represent the thoughts and feelings of larger bodies of people. Furthermore, every impersonal historical trend has *physical* correlates which lend themselves very well to visual presentation. In fact, it is hard to escape the conclusion that if television producers regularly avoid certain categories of information and thus incline towards one particular social theory, an explanation must be sought not in the potentialities of the medium but in their own attitudes and ideologies. Whether these are formed within the broadcasting institutions or in the wider community is a matter for further consideration; at all events, the causes are extrinsic to the medium.

A frequent criticism of the 'great man' approach to social explanation emphasizes its inadequacy rather than any outright errors. It selects some facts but neglects others which may be crucial for a complete interpretation of events. In failing to 'locate' the actions of individuals within a social context, it cannot help us understand why an individual should act in a certain way or why his actions have certain effects. The 'intrinsic media characteristics' argument suffers from similar shortcomings. It does not begin to explain variations in the subject matter and conceptual orientation of television programmes and, more importantly, it fails to establish causal links between a society and the messages it generates.

References

Britain: an Official Handbook (1972 ed.) London, HMSO.

BURNHAM, J. (1942) *The Managerial Revolution*, New York and London, Putnam.

CASTLES, F. G., MURRAY, D. J. and POTTER, D. C. (eds.) (1971) *Decisions, Organizations and Society*, Harmondsworth, Penguin.

CHAPMAN, R. A. (1969) *Decision Making*, London, Routledge and Kegan Paul.

HANSON, A. H. and WALLES, M. (1970) *Governing Britain*, London, Fontana.

MICHELS, R. (1958) *Political Parties*, Glencoe, Illinois, Free Press.

MOSCA, G. (1939) *The Ruling Class*, New York, McGraw-Hill.

PARETO, V. (1935) *The Mind and Society* (Treatise of General Society), New York, Harcourt Brace.

PARRY, G. (1969) *Political Elites*, London, Allen and Unwin.

REID, G. L. and ALLEN, K. (1970) *Nationalized Industries*, Harmondsworth, Penguin.

WRIGHT MILLS, C. (1956) *The Power Elite*, New York, Oxford University Press.

Acknowledgements

Grateful acknowledgement is made to the following sources for material used in this part:

Allen and Unwin for D. VITAL, *The Making of British Foreign Policy*; Clarendon Press for S. E. FINER, 'The Federation of British Industries' in 'The Confederation of British Industry', reprinted in Block VI of *Decision making in Britain* and for W. P. GRANT and D. MARSH, 'The Confederation of British Industries' in *Political Studies*, Vol. XIX, No. 4, reprinted in Block VI of *Decision making in Britain*; André Deutsch for LORD STRANG, *Home and Abroad*; Fontana for A. H. HANSON and M. WALLES, *Governing Britain*; Hutchinson for D. G. T. WILLIAMS, 'The law of public order in Britain' in *Keeping the Peace*, reprinted in Block II of *Decision making in Britain*; Penguin Books for D. THOMSON, *England in the Twentieth Century*; Random House for P. SEABURY, *Power, Freedom and Diplomacy: The Foreign Policy of the United States of America*; Times Newspaper Limited for J. DAVIES and for P. JAY in *The Business Times*, 1 May 1971.

Part 3
The social sciences and contributing disciplines

Section 1
Advancing understanding of the social sciences
David J. Murray

Section 2
Disciplinary themes
Andrew Blowers
Ruth Finnegan
David J. Murray
Ray Thomas

Part 3   Contents

Section 1
Advancing understanding of the social sciences

At the beginning of the foundation year social science course *Understanding Society* five radio programmes were devoted to introducing the social sciences, and at the end of this second level social science course this note is intended to comment on how, in broad terms, *Decision making in Britain* has contributed to advancing your understanding of the social sciences. At the end of this section you should be able, therefore, to state major characteristics of the social sciences and explain how the course *Decision making in Britain* has illustrated them.

In commenting on its contribution, this section will place the course in the context of the general features of the social sciences as outlined at the beginning of the foundation course *Understanding Society*. Some of you did not take that course and it could scarcely be expected that those who did would be able to cast their minds back and recall the content of each of the first five radio programmes, so I will begin by summarizing the main points made. Those who wish to do so will be able to listen to the programmes themselves, which are available on cassettes, in the usual way.

The first five radio programmes in the D100 course began by outlining basic characteristics of the social sciences as a whole, and four features were distinguished. First of all, something that is quite fundamental in the social sciences is that they represent a search for systematic explanations about social life. Rather than looking for a different explanation for some occurrence as wholly unique, there is a concern in the social sciences to find explanations that would cover many cases, and to express these explanations as theory. 'Even if we do appeal to different causes on different occasions we always assume that behind them there's some more general principle or that they in turn are instances of some general principle. And this is because we try to back up our explanations with some kind of theory' (Ryan, Radio Programme D100 1).

Secondly, it is presented as a characteristic that attention in the social sciences is often directed to problems of immediate social concern. Yet, and this is a third point and another quite fundamental one, the social sciences are empirical rather than normative. Instead of being concerned to say what 'ought' to be they are preoccupied with what actually 'is'. 'Empirical social theory which is what occupies contemporary social scientists to a large extent is mostly aimed at telling us more carefully, in more detail, with greater theoretical understanding how we actually do behave rather than giving us instructions as to how we ought to behave' (Ryan, Radio Programme D100 1). What helps to increase the importance of this distinction in the social sciences is that much attention is given to practical matters of concern. Simply because of the nature of these matters particular emphasis is laid on their empirical nature.

As a further characteristic, the social sciences have developed disciplines. In general terms the process by which disciplines have developed is presented as being the result, to begin with, of increased methodological sophistication, which produces a more self conscious identity among exponents of the discipline, and this in its turn prompts a more precise demarcation of fields of activity. There is, therefore, an internal dynamic in the development of disciplines which is not prompted simply by the particular problems or concerns that initiated enquiry, but once a discipline becomes established there is a concentration of attention on a limited range of phenomena which enables breakthroughs to be made in these particular areas. 'Once you've got a well defined field with some body of theory which the practitioners in that field accept, then you know what kind of observations you've got to make, you know what kinds of facts to pile up. And I think it is in a sense one of the key features of the social sciences that this process has over the last few years been gathering momentum . . .' (Ryan, Radio Programme D100 1). Yet this very concentration prompts a questioning of what underlies the theory in accordance with which all the facts are piled up. And the example discussed was of the way economics was built up on an assumption of how men behave in which the political, social and psychological background was held constant. 'For example in the 1930s a lot of industrial sociology discovered that you could offer people higher wages in various factories and production just didn't go up at all. Now obviously the economist would expect that it would because if you offer higher prices you generally get more goods, in this case work, but nothing of the sort happened. Now at that point you obviously have to begin to ask social psychologists, industrial sociologists and the like why it is that the assumptions on which economics rest on some occasions actually break down.' (Ryan, Radio Programme D100 1.)

Disciplines, however, produce a concentration on certain facets of social life, and interdisciplinary enquiry is prompted not simply when assumptions are questioned on which disciplinary theory is built, but because many problems or topics are not capable of being systematically explained on the basis of existing and established social science disciplines. As a result, 'There is one very important dilemma that we have to face from the beginning, which is that specialization does seem essential to making progress, particularly technical progress, in any academic discipline, and yet to be of practical use some sort of interdisciplinary understanding also seems absolutely essential. Now it seems to me that in spite of our best efforts there's no such thing as a cut and dried solution here.' (Ryan, Radio Programme D100 1.)

The social sciences have, therefore, built up a body of knowledge about society – or rather about particular facets of society, ones often related to what are, or have been, problems – in pursuit of systematic explanations founded on empirical enquiry. What the social sciences have to offer is this body of knowledge, and a method and approach. In the second of the radio programmes in D100 some further characteristics of this method and approach were identified. Presented in a simple – maybe over-simplified – way this involved an initial appreciation of assumed ideas, subsequent exploration, and, as a culmination, systematic enquiry on the basis of testing an hypothesis.

Everyone starts with a body of knowledge about society, and often this will reflect conventional wisdom in the particular culture. Sir William Armstrong in a later programme instanced a nineteenth century attitude towards the poor: 'It was held a hundred years or so ago that the poor were poor because of their own fault, that there was a fecklessness in some people which just made them poor, and the actions of society towards them were conditioned by that view of them.' (Armstrong, Radio Programme D100 4.) A starting point for any social scientist is an attempt to identify assumed ideas, both one's own and those in the conventional wisdom of the society; indeed the desire to pursue enquiry may be prompted by a realization that assumed theory is inadequate to explain reality. 'We all have a body of theory, and that is what we come to the world with, and when we explore the world, what we do is suddenly find that theory doesn't quite fit. It isn't theory development, it's realizing that the theories we already possess are in some sense inadequate.' (Castles, Radio Programme D100 2.)

From this first realization enquiry leads on to what was characterized in the programme as the exploratory stage, in which the aim is to familiarize oneself with an area of investigation, discovering questions one wants to ask and formulating them in an appropriate way. At this point enquiry can lead on to drawing up and testing a specific hypothesis about some particular problem within a field as a preliminary to more adequate explanations of that aspect of human behaviour. In this work of investigating a hypothesis documentary material is used, and the enquirer may in addition 'go out and collect (information) for himself' (Drake, Radio Programme D100 3) using some form of direct observation, social survey, or experiment.

This account of the social sciences came at the beginning of the foundation social science course, but it is as relevant to an appreciation of the course *Decision making in Britain* as it is for *Understanding Society*, for to the question of where this course takes you in terms of advancing your understanding of the social sciences, one answer is that, at a general level, it illustrates the social sciences as characterized in the foundation year.

The course *Decision making in Britain* exemplifies many of the points made in the abstract in those first radio programmes. It has quite clearly been looking for systematic explanation, in the sense that it has been seeking to move from particular instances to generalizations about decision making in sectors and in society as a whole. From the beginning it has differentiated normative and empirical analyses of decision making in society, and emphasized the way the course has been preoccupied with empirical enquiry.

In relation to the development and nature of disciplines and the stimuli for interdisciplinary study the course has made no direct contribution to illustrating the way disciplines have emerged and characteristically operated. *Decision making in Britain* has been an interdisciplinary course, not a single discipline or multidisciplinary one. What it has done is indirectly to illustrate certain of the points made about the development of disciplines and directly to illustrate the inspirations for interdisciplinary enquiry. The course has in the first place derived in part from a questioning of assumptions that have underlain work in certain disciplines. Most strikingly and explicitly this was indicated by H. A. Simon, both in the second radio programme of the course and in the article from which an extract is provided in the Reader. His own enquiry into how people do in fact decide derived in part from a questioning of that assumption made by economists about man's decision making behaviour to which Ryan referred and which is quoted above. It is equally the case that Simon's enquiries result from a similar questioning of assumptions about decision making behaviour underlying the discipline of public administration. Starting as a student of public administration he questioned the characteristics of 'administrative man' on which public administration theory was built in the same way that he questioned the characteristics of 'economic man'. 'The theory of administration is concerned with how an organization should be constructed and operated in order to accomplish its work efficiently. A fundamental principle of administration, which follows almost immediately from the rational character of "good" administration, is that among several alternatives involving the same expenditure the one should always be selected which leads to the greatest accomplishment of administrative objectives; and among several alternatives that lead to the same accomplishment the one should be selected which involves the least expenditure. Since this "principle of efficiency" is characteristic of any activity that attempts rationally to maximize the attainment of certain ends with the use of scarce means, it is characteristic of economic theory as it is of administrative theory. The "administrative man" takes his place alongside the classical "economic man".' (Simon, 1957.)[1] A considerable body of the theoretical material and empirical data presented in

1   The initial questioning arose out of an attempt at measuring efficiency in municipal activities. See Ridley and Simon (1943), preface.

the course derives from a questioning of these basic assumptions in economics and public administration. As was made clear in Block I (Part 4, Section 3, p. 161) this is equally true of political science where much of the material used in this course has derived from the questioning of assumptions about the state as the focal point in a study of political activity.

Yet the body of social science knowledge drawn on in this course does not derive simply from this questioning of assumptions underlying general theory; decision making is also one of those topics that has because of its nature prompted interdisciplinary enquiry. As Simon indicated in the second radio programme it has developed as a point of concentration for social scientists drawn from a range of disciplines. Decision making has characteristically demanded an interdisciplinary approach.

While exemplifying points made about basic features of the social sciences the course has also illustrated the strategy of enquiry which the social sciences were characterized as following. Encouraging an awareness of assumed attitudes about decision making in Britain was the initial objective which was set out for you to pursue in Block I of the course, and the course then proceeded through an exploratory phase to your investigating and testing hypotheses, first a limited one in Block V, and then a more wide ranging one in Block VI, where you had to extend the methods used from a consideration of documentary and related non-written sources and direct observation, to ones that involved going out and collecting your own data using in this instance a questionnaire. The course has in other words built up in a way that illustrates the account presented in the radio programmes in the *Understanding Society* course.

Quite apart, therefore, from the substantive social science knowledge acquired in this course, the course should have conveyed a deeper appreciation of the nature of the social sciences. In its practice it has illustrated the character and importance of distinguishing features – the pursuit of systematic generalization and the emphasis on empirical rather than normative enquiry. It has exemplified the way an interdisciplinary approach emerges to question and complement disciplinary pursuits. The course has, in its construction, indicated the approach of seeking to verbalize assumed and implicit models and theories, of undertaking an exploratory stage to gain an understanding about an area of investigation, and of advancing knowledge of one aspect of an area by setting up and exploring a hypothesis. And finally it has self-consciously assumed methods of building up empirical data whether from documentary or related sources, or by interviews on the basis of a schedule.

In explaining the contribution of this course to an appreciation of the social sciences it would however be a mistake to leave the impression that, even at the general level at which the nature of the social sciences has been discussed, there is broad agreement among social scientists. In fact much is in dispute. There is considerable debate, for example, about the extent to which a search for systematic explanations can usefully and validly go, and about what the social sciences can do now in their present state of development. This course has reflected one point of view – the point of view that was expressed in the fourth of those radio programmes to which I have already referred. Andrew Schonfield put his point of view in saying '. . . in the early stages of social sciences demonstrating that certain accepted prejudices won't work – this is an immensely powerful tool . . . but so far as demonstrating positively what persons ought to do, who have power and authority, I think we're at an immensely primitive stage . . .' (Schonfield, Radio Programme D100 4). Sir William Armstrong went on at a later point to develop a related idea: '. . . I think it is a very important point that has begun to emerge out of our increasing use of social science methods. It is the point of the ranges of uncertainty. In the early days of this sort of thing we tended to think that we could make precise predictions and we had at the back of our minds rather precise formulae ... but as we have gone on, we have seen that it is really much more important to display the range of uncertainty and to allow people to draw their own sensible conclusions from that.' (Armstrong, Radio Programme D100 4.) This point of view is one that you will recognize in the course: but it is only one point of view and an alternative opinion which displays greater confidence in the immediate capabilities of the social sciences as a science of prediction and explanation, and in consequence concentrates on the development of high level generalizations that accurately and truly interrelate social phenomena, has strong support among social scientists. This view too you will have found reflected at certain points in this course.

There is much debate about other features of the social sciences and about their methods and approaches – argument about when to proceed from exploratory studies to the investigation of a hypothesis, disagreement about the relative value of different methods, social surveys for instance as against direct observation. This has not been a course in the philosophy of the social sciences nor directly in methods and techniques, and in saying that the course illustrates basic characteristics of the social sciences as set out at the beginning of the course *Understanding Society* it must also be appreciated that there is creative debate proceeding about the social sciences, and this course as an illustration of the social sciences inevitably – it could not do otherwise – reflects particular standpoints more than others.

References

RIDLEY, C. E. and SIMON, H. A. (1943) *Measuring Municipal Activities*, 2nd edition, Chicago, International City Managers' Association.

SIMON, H. A. (1957) *Administrative Behavior: A Study of Decision-Making Processes in Administrative Organizations*, 2nd edition, New York, Macmillan, pp. 38–39.

Section 2
Disciplinary themes

1   A concluding note on geography and decision making

The specifically geographical themes of the course were introduced in Block I (Part 4, Section 3.5). These were elaborated in the geographical contributions to the sectoral blocks. The issues raised by those contributions that are relevant to the major questions about decision making posed in the course have been considered as separate notes in Part 2 of this block. Here attention is confined to those aspects of geographical enquiry which are illuminated in the course.

In the section by Jones on 'Agricultural innovation and farmer decision making' (Block III) spatial factors play a relatively small part. The *physical environment* defines the outer limits within which an innovation may be diffused. *Geographical distance* is seen as a factor that can influence the pattern of adoption, especially in the early stages of innovation diffusion. Spatial factors are regarded along with all other relevant factors as providing the total environment of decision making. In its approach this section illustrates two characteristics which modern geography shares with other social sciences. First it deals with individual behaviour. The *behavioural* approach in geography has developed most rapidly in those areas where the explanations of aggregative theories are least adequate. Secondly, it is concerned with a *process*, in this case with the process of innovation diffusion. Geographers have begun to concentrate more on processes in order to explain the spatial patterns with which they are primarily concerned.

This traditional concern with *patterns* is evident from the other two geographical sections in the course. 'Power stations – a study of the spatial implications of decisions' (Block IV) is a detailed empirical study. Apart from its relevance to the general decisions on fuel policy it is a free-standing study unrelated to any particular model or theory. The emphasis here, unlike that of many locational studies, is not upon the discovery or description of a pattern, for the location of power stations linked by grid lines is taken as a starting point. The central concern here is the explanation of pattern. This is achieved by evaluating the relevant factors. Fuel, transmission, and markets comprise the factors which determine locational strategy while amenity or water supply may condition the actual siting of power stations or grid lines. Although economic factors provide the basis of locational policy, decisions are inevitably shaped by other forces. This leads us on to a consideration of the social costs and benefits of locational decisions.

The social implications of geographical patterns are inherent in Part 2, 'Regional disparities in the health sector' in Block V. The patterns described provide ample scope for tantalizing speculation. By emphasizing regional disparities the essay seems to imply that the underlying causes may be found in differences in the physical environment, whether natural or man made. Such differences may most likely be explained by the distribution of income and employment characteristics. This critical role of economic factors is established by inference, for no explicit explanation of regional disparities is offered. Instead the essay attempts to discover and analyse spatial patterns of health. In doing so it brings out two further aspects of modern geographical enquiry:

(a)   The role of the region in geography. Traditionally the 'regional method'

(Block I Introduction Part 4, Section 3, 5.2) was used as the basis of geographical synthesis. Today regions are no longer regarded as discrete entities but as areal data units for *regional analysis*. The spatial scale chosen will vary according to the problem being tackled though data availability may be a further constraint.

(b)   The importance of *quantification* in modern geography. Not only are particular statistical techniques introduced but the problems associated with them are discussed. Among these are variations in the size and type of statistical units which render comparison difficult; the lack of data for certain variables or at certain spatial scales; and the problems associated with random sampling procedures. At every stage in the statistical testing of a hypothesis choices as to method must be made. The validity of the results is as dependent on the quality of the choices made as it is upon the quantity of data available.

Although each of these essays has a distinctive approach and one that is interdisciplinary in character, taken together they convey a tangible impression of the nature and method of modern geography. It is a discipline which focuses on the spatial dimension and expresses it in terms of locations and interactions between them and the areas within which they occur. These either singly or together assume spatial patterns which geographers discover, describe, and explain. Explanation may involve the investigation of a particular process or the attributes of several. The investigation of spatial patterns and processes may broaden the scope of social enquiry and contribute to better informed decision making.

2   The place of sociology in the course

The place of sociology in this course may well not be immediately obvious. This section is designed to elucidate in what sense I consider sociology has contributed to the course.

One possible reaction to this course would be to suggest that it contains no sociology as such at all. This would be an understandable reaction and there is a sense in which there is some truth in it. For it is true that sociology is not presented and taught in this course as a subject or discipline *in itself* – at most, it *contributes* to the discussion of certain questions in an interdisciplinary context. As you will have noticed the main sectors to which it has contributed are those of health and public order (Blocks II and V), but even there the discipline of sociology is not elaborated for its own sake nor presented in separable and distinct units of the course.[1]

Even the ways in which sociology contributes to the course may seem to some rather 'unsociological'. This assessment would seem the reasonable one to those who regard sociology as essentially consisting of sociological theory with an emphasis on specialist concepts and theory building and/or the history of sociological theory. So it must be stated straight away that although theoretical sociology is indeed one important aspect of sociology – *how* important an aspect is a matter of controversy – it is not the side of sociology emphasized in this course. Thus, though there are naturally parts of this course which bear some relation to current controversies in sociological theory,[2] it is only fair to say that you should not expect on completing this course to have gained a mastery of the specialist vocabulary or problems within the broad field of sociological theory.[3]

There are, however, other sides to sociology. There are of course difficulties

1   As it was, for example, in the Social Science Foundation Course (D100).

2   Discussed below, p. 92.

3   For this, you can turn to *The Sociological Perspective* (D283).

in separating off theoretical sociology from empirical or descriptive sociology (after all, how could one make an empirical study of the facts without involving some theory, if only implicitly?) but, accepting that total separation is impossible, it would be true to say that the emphasis in this course is more towards the empirical than the theoretical end of the continuum. In Block II, for instance, the aim is not to build up theoretical formulations about, say, order in society but to try to find out just how policemen or judges behave, and why they do what they do, and insofar as a theoretical model enters in, its test and aim is taken to be how far it illuminates and aids description and explanation of such down to earth facts as the behaviour of magistrates on the bench, or policemen on the beat, rather than theoretical elaboration in abstract terms or a historical account of the various theories on such topics. This relatively[1] more empirical emphasis is an eminently reputable one within sociology and some authorities would even maintain that it characterizes the more fruitful growing points within the subject – but it must be repeated that it *is* only one aspect and that this course does *not* attempt to deal with sociological theory as such or with the intellectual history of the subject.

Of course an emphasis on empirical sociology can be directed to very many different topics. There is no one part of the world which is somehow inherently 'sociological' in nature and thus demands that sociologists should concentrate their attention on that bit of nature and no other. It is thus perfectly open for sociologists to take as their topic 'decision making in Britain', and this is what has been done in this course. It is true that the subject does not happen to coincide with one of the conventional topics taught as sociology courses in universities up and down the country, nor is it one that the sociologists among the course team were themselves taught as undergraduates. Nevertheless it is a broad area of study which is now becoming increasingly established not only for political scientists but for social scientists generally – and, among them, sociologists. Apart therefore from its being somewhat newer than some fields, there is nothing about the topic of 'decision making in Britain' which makes it less viable as a subject for sociological study than more traditional specialisms.

A number of the more established topics for either university courses and/or research in sociology are, however, touched on in the course and it may be of interest to note some of these briefly, not least because they make it easier to take further some aspect that particularly interests you. Much of the public order block (Block II) falls within what could be broadly described as the sociology of law, including within this some overlap with criminology and/or the sociology of deviance; insights are also touched on here from the study of law and social order by social anthropologists. In Block III, much of the discussion about the spread of innovations in agriculture could, in some circles at least, be taught under the general heading of 'rural sociology' (or even, perhaps, the sociological study of 'social change') whereas much of the block dealing with health (Block V) coincides with 'medical sociology' and also involves some overlap with topics sometimes taught under the heading of 'social administration'. 'Political sociology' (discussed and defined in Block I, pp. 160–1) not only plays some part in structuring the course generally, but is particularly stressed in the Reader (Parts II and III especially) and in much of the material in this block. In addition, some of the discussion and practice of collecting data in Block VI might elsewhere have appeared in a course specifically on 'Methods of social research' (or some such title), whereas the sections on the interpretation of evidence could be elaborated in courses on methodology and the philosophy of the social sciences. Though a summary list like this runs the risk of suggesting that the sociology in the course is all bits and pieces, it is

1   *Relatively* – because it is in practice impossible to separate off 'empirical' and 'theoretical' completely.

worth repeating that many classifications (e.g. 'rural sociology' or 'medical sociology') are primarily matters of convention, subject to variation, and that there is in fact a clear and integrated focus in this course on which the sociologists have concentrated: that is, 'decision making in Britain'.

A further advantage of proceeding in this way is that it gives you the opportunity to look at aspects of the subject which may be of great interest and importance, but do not happen to have become established as one of the conventional subjects for undergraduate sociology courses. The sociological study of, for instance, legal institutions, which is emphasized in this course, has till recently been a relatively neglected and disorganized subject pursued by individual researchers but not much taught as an undergraduate subject in universities; it is now an expanding field and attracting increasing interest.

Something must also be said about the approach of sociology in this course. For since, as has been suggested, there is no specific subject matter by which sociology is to be differentiated from other disciplines, its definition is likely to be at least partly in terms of a distinctive *approach*.

This is no easy question to pursue and any rigorous discussion of the problem would be controversial, highly complex and not suitable for elaboration here. However, it may be illuminating, in the context of how sociology has contributed in this course, to quote Berger's brief description of sociology as 'the art of mistrust' (Berger, 1966, p. 42) and the similar remarks by Burns about how sociology 'operates . . . by questioning assumptions which seem to be made by people, and especially by people in authority in education, law, politics and so forth, about the behaviour of people' (Burns, 1970, p. 59). The way sociologists are often not content with accepting conventional assumptions or explanations at their face value but want to probe further comes out at various places in the course. For example, it is argued that it is not enough just to accept the judges' view (Block II) or the doctors' view (Block V) of their role or their selection processes, or even their behaviour. It is true that their view is certainly part of reality which must be taken serious account of, but it is not enough to stop there. A sociologist also wants to ask about other factors which may come in, or about other possible analyses or descriptions of their behaviour. Again, as the sociologists have stressed throughout the course, the common assumptions about the significance of formal structure or about, say, the validity of the instrumental theory of administration (see for example Block I, p. 160) need to be questioned by reference, among other things, to people's actual behaviour. This probing and questioning approach to how people really behave on the ground may sometimes appear overcritical or cynical to those studied,[1] precisely because it involves questioning certain perhaps comfortable assumptions.

Within this general emphasis on questioning conventional ideas there are certain emphases that, while hardly sociological dogmas, crop up frequently enough in the more sociological sections of this course to deserve particular attention here. First, there is the interest in the hidden implications behind people's actions. For example it emerges in Blocks II, III and V that while nurses or farmers or policemen may not be explicitly aware of the ideologies or assumed explanations which underlie many of their actions, these may be discoverable by a sociologist and used to explain what they do, or even to draw up rules about likely behaviour – and yet the actors themselves may not be aware of such rules. Again, the consequences of certain actions may not be realized by the actors themselves and yet they may have unanticipated results of the utmost importance. In the public order block, for instance, it is suggested that the *cumulative* effect of a number of small decisions by individual policemen or magistrates may arguably have results for the society at large out of all

---

1   Note, for instance, the sensitivity of the judiciary to research, as discussed in Radio Programme 5.

proportion to what could have been anticipated by the participants themselves, and a similar point could be made in the context of the acceptance of certain innovations by farmers. Similarly it may not be obvious to the framers of a particular law or planners of a particular hospital structure that the process of the actual *administration* of this rule may cause it to have certain unanticipated results, perhaps the opposite of those intended by the planners.

A second interest pursued by many sociologists – and one which particularly fits with the aspect of *political sociology*[1] in this course – is in the overall social structure of the society, particularly in the sense of the distribution of power in society. Thus questions about the impact of certain actions and institutions on the class hierarchy, and vice versa, are considered as of great significance; there too it may be the unanticipated consequences and implications that assume greatest importance. This aspect is pursued particularly in Part III of the Reader and in certain sections of Block VIII.

The last two points to be mentioned are perhaps of especial significance for what has turned out to be the particular emphasis of much of the sociology in this course. There is, thirdly, the interest in the *interaction* of individuals and groups. Perhaps the clearest example of this is in Roth's article (Block V, Section 2) in which he discusses the interaction and bargaining process between patients and staff in a tuberculosis hospital. But it also enters constantly into other of the more sociological parts of the course, e.g. the emphasis by Cain and Finnegan on the interaction between police and public (Block II, Part 4, Sections 4 and 6) or Strauss' emphasis on the interaction which helps to make up the 'negotiated order' of the hospital (Reader, pp. 103 ff). This stress on the actual interaction of people on the ground can be contrasted in a general way with the kind of sociological approach which concentrates on such concepts as 'social structure' or 'social system' and often operates at a somewhat more abstract and generalized level.

Finally – and closely connected with the previous point – there is the sociologist's interest in this course in the *meaning* people attach to actions or institutions, on their *perceptions* of the world.[2] This comes out, for instance, in the various papers by Power, Finnegan, Strauss, Roth and Boswell (mainly in Blocks II and V). This again can be contrasted broadly with the type of sociological approach which lays more stress on function or external system than on the subjective meanings people attach to things.[3]

This interesting question cannot be elaborated with any adequacy here but it must be pointed out that how far sociologists should lay particular stress on these aspects is currently a matter for controversy within sociology. In particular, there is controversy between those who would wish to take up a position on what has been termed the 'symbolic interactionist' and/or 'phenomenological' wing of sociology as opposed to those (till recently more established in Britain) who emphasize overall structure, system or function. While it would be exaggerated to say either that these two approaches were self-evidently fully distinct, opposed to one another, or that this course embraces anything like a fully 'interactionist' perspective, it is only honest to say that much of the sociology in the course does tend somewhat towards the interactionist side of the controversy.[4]

1   See discussion of this in Block I, pp. 160–61.

2   Block VII also includes some interesting discussion of the significance of people's *perceptions*.

3   This possible contrast is discussed more fully – indeed to some extent taken as the key controversy – in *The Sociological Perspective* (D283); see especially Units 5–8.

4   Since there is not space to enter into the complexities of this argument here, students who wish to pursue this question further are referred to *The Sociological Perspective* (D283) and to its accompanying Reader (Thompson and Tunstall, eds., 1971), especially the extracts by Dawe and Silverman reprinted in that Reader.

This interactionist emphasis does not have everything its own way, however. You will have noticed, for example, the stress on the formal structure in Kogan's paper (Block V, Part 5, Section 1), the more pluralist model by and large assumed in the set book by Willcocks (1967), and the far from interactionist approach in much of the political sociology in Parts II and III of the Reader. In particular it will be noticed that the paper on the goal seeking model in Block IV, Part 7, represents a very different approach within sociology. The model discussed in that paper is one that has been used extensively in certain branches of sociology, most notably in the field of organizational sociology.

How the central questions in the course are answered is partly a matter for individual interpretation. As will be obvious from the juxtapositions indicated in the last few paragraphs, there is no set 'sociological' answer or discovery in the course which leads to authoritative conclusions. However, if I was forced to state in a sentence or two the single main direction in which I myself would consider much of the more sociological sections seemed to be tending, I would suggest that the main aspect to emerge is how far decisions seem to be diffused throughout the society. At first sight it might seem that decisions are made at the centre or by those accepted as possessing 'power' – but in practice, largely because of the way even administration involves discretion right along the line, decisions are constantly being made in minor but cumulatively important ways right through the society. Thus, while both the formal structure and the many unintended consequences and implications of people's actions certainly form a significant background, these can be regarded not as the first or sole explanations, but as constraints within which people operate and manipulate and make decisions. The 'negotiated order(s)' in our society is/are something constantly created and recreated by ourselves, not something imposed and immutably 'given'; and decisions are thus constantly, and at all levels, being made and remade in contemporary Britain.

Doubtless you will already have noticed that this sort of 'conclusion', which I have argued emerges in several of the more sociological sections of the course, bears some relation to the particular stress I mentioned earlier both on interaction and on people's meaning and perceptions – i.e. the emphasis on the more interactionist side of sociology. It could indeed be strongly argued that this particular conclusion was already built into the investigation because of the particular theoretical framework adopted by many of the sociologists on the central course team. Thus trying to look for empirical conclusions has (as I hinted earlier) led us back to theory after all. Descriptions of the facts turn out to be difficult without either a model or something approaching it (for example the 'negotiated order' model elaborated in Block V), just as interpretation and assumption are always built into our perception of the evidence.

Whether this *invalidates* the kinds of conclusions to which many, though not all of the more sociological sections seem to be tending, or whether it merely means that we must be wary of stating them as unchallengeable dogma – this must be left to you to decide. For myself, let me admit that I think the game is worth the candle: in other words that, admitting all the theoretical assumptions and subjective interpretation behind what I have suggested as a sort of conclusion, I still want to hold to the picture of decision making as diffused through society as being one very significant part of the truth, one well worth being elucidated by sociologists. You may well disagree – just as a number of sociologists (including some who have contributed to this course) would probably query the amount of emphasis I have laid on this aspect. But I think that there would at least be fairly general agreement that this is one important aspect of society and of decision making (even if not the only possible one) about which it is entirely appropriate for sociologists to enquire.

3   Political science: disciplinary themes

The political science threads running through this course were introduced and explained in the first block of the course. At this stage no more is called for than a brief recapitulation of the points made there as a reminder of where this course fits into a developing study of political science.

In Block I, Part 4, the political science threads running through this course were identified as being four in number. First, there was the obvious point that this course had concentrated on Britain, and as such the course complemented the work which some of you did in the foundation year. It forms part of the study of political science to acquire a certain level of information about governments in societies. In the foundation year attention was directed to political systems in non-industrial societies and to government in the United States, and this course has added some understanding of government in Britain.

This course has also aimed to carry further the understanding of politics in society gained in the foundation course *Understanding Society* through its concentration on decision making. Political scientists have moved away from the study of the state as they have discarded the assumption that political activity is simply activity pertaining to the state, and they have sought instead an alternative point of attention. As abstract definitions of politics have been developed, so there has been a need to operationalize these abstract ideas, and to identify phenomena which can be studied empirically. The attention given to decision making is one result, for the assumption has been made that any exercise of power requires a decision, and thus in pursuing decisions and decision makers the student of politics is concentrating on what lies at the heart of politics. By this stage in the course you will have reached conclusions about advantages and shortcomings in this assumption and about merits and disadvantages of such an approach to the empirical study of politics. You should be able in other words to answer the question 'what are the benefits, and what the problems, of seeking an understanding of politics in society through a focus on decision making?'

In addition to these two threads, this course has both implicitly and explicitly given consideration to administration. Attention has been directed to the institutions of public administration in Britain and to the nature of the administrative function. In so doing the course has both drawn on the study of public administration and provided an introduction to aspects of this discipline (or as some would have it this sub-discipline of political science). In political science there has traditionally been a division between politics and administration, and while, in the foundation year, attention was focused on the politics dimension, in this course considerable attention has been given to administration. In each sector a survey has been made of the institutions of public administration, and running right through the course have been those issues, presented at the beginning, of the extent to which administrative institutions are involved in the political process, and of whether the instrumental theory of administration holds. Are the institutions of public administration outside the realm of politics; and can the administrative process in Britain be regarded as a relatively mechanical process of carrying out major policy decisions taken through the political process?

In direct conflict with what might be derived from an instrumental theory of administration, political sociologists would postulate that those staffing the public administration – the bureaucracy – in Britain form part of a ruling class or ruling élite. Political sociologists in the tradition of Gaetano Mosca have regarded the bureaucracy in modern western societies as an integral part of a ruling class or ruling élite, and in postulating such a role for the bureaucracy in Britain, a directly contrary point of view is being presented to what might be assumed from certain writings in public administration. The place of the public administration or bureaucracy in the decision making process in Britain is an issue with which you have been directly concerned in this course. You have been exploring the formal structural model which assigns a primarily instrumental role to the institutions of the public administration, and equally you have been considering alternative models of which a ruling class and ruling élite are two.

To present my personal conclusions on these questions would be inappropriate, not least because some of you will be submitting an essay as part of TMA D203 10 which directly considers the points raised in the two previous paragraphs. What is apposite is to draw your attention to the fact that there have been a series of political science threads running through the course, and while you have been pursuing the central objectives of the course you have also been gathering evidence and coming to conclusions on issues that have an immediate significance for these disciplinary threads. Conclusions reached on major issues in the course can be recast as conclusions to important issues in the developing discipline of political science.

4   The place of economics in the course

Some traditionally minded economists would not regard this course as having made much of a contribution to the understanding of the subject. This is because much of economics consists of abstract reasoning on the basis of simplified assumptions which may have little empirical justification. As H. A. Simon said in the second radio programme of the course, 'acceptance of the assumptions of classical economics allows us to answer many questions from an armchair without ever having to go out to look at the world'.

The economics contributions to this course were not designed to advance this kind of theory. Instead the approach adopted is empirical. The aim in Blocks III and IV was to define those objectives of decision making in agriculture and nationalized industries which can be expressed in economic terms, to discuss how those objectives could be measured and achieved, and to discuss the extent to which those objectives are consistent with other objectives.

One of the things you should have learnt from these parts of the course is that economics does not offer straightforward answers. An apparently simple concept like economic efficiency is not easily definable or measurable. The assumption that producing more food in Britain will help to produce a more positive balance of trade cannot be justified in terms of the complexities of the real world any more than it can be in theory. Neither commercial success nor marginal cost pricing are by themselves an adequate basis for economic policy for the nationalized industries. There are no simple criteria by which the investment decisions in nationalized industries can be appraised.

But, more positively, it is hoped that the economics contribution has enabled you to use many of the conceptual tools of economics to provide an understanding of the decision making problems faced in government policy for agriculture, the nationalized industries or indeed other sectors. You should be able to discuss these problems in terms of alternative measures of efficiency, in terms of the economies of scale and the economies of joint production, in terms of the theory of comparative advantage, in terms of rates of return from capital, and most important, in terms of social cost and benefit.

References

BERGER, P. (1966) *Invitation to Sociology*, Harmondsworth, Penguin.

BURNS, T. (1970) 'Sociological explanation' as reprinted in EMMET, D. and MACINTYRE, A. (eds.), *Sociological Theory and Philosophical Analysis*, London, Macmillan.

THOMPSON, K. and TUNSTALL, J. (eds.) (1971) *Sociological Perspectives*, Harmondsworth, Penguin.

WILLCOCKS, A. J. (1967) *The Creation of the National Health Service*, London, Routledge and Kegan Paul.

Acknowledgements

Grateful acknowledgement is made to the following sources for material used in this part:

Macmillan for T. BURNS, 'Sociological explanation', reprinted in D. EMMET and A. MACINTYRE (eds.) *Sociological Theory and Philosophical Analysis*; Penguin Books for P. BERGER (1966) *Invitation to Sociology*.

Part 4
Developing further the study of
decision making in Britain

3   Political science: disciplinary themes

The political science threads running through this course were introduced
and explained in the first block of the course. At this stage no more is called
for than a brief recapitulation of the points made there as a reminder of where
this course fits into a developing study of political science.

In Block I, Part 4, the political science threads running through this course
were identified as being four in number. First, there was the obvious point
that this course had concentrated on Britain, and as such the course complemented the work which some of you did in the foundation year. It forms
part of the study of political science to acquire a certain level of information
about governments in societies. In the foundation year attention was directed
to political systems in non-industrial societies and to government in the United
States, and this course has added some understanding of government in
Britain.

This course has also aimed to carry further the understanding of politics in
society gained in the foundation course *Understanding Society* through its concentration on decision making. Political scientists have moved away from the
study of the state as they have discarded the assumption that political activity
is simply activity pertaining to the state, and they have sought instead an
alternative point of attention. As abstract definitions of politics have been
developed, so there has been a need to operationalize these abstract ideas, and
to identify phenomena which can be studied empirically. The attention given
to decision making is one result, for the assumption has been made that any
exercise of power requires a decision, and thus in pursuing decisions and
decision makers the student of politics is concentrating on what lies at the heart
of politics. By this stage in the course you will have reached conclusions about
advantages and shortcomings in this assumption and about merits and disadvantages of such an approach to the empirical study of politics. You should
be able in other words to answer the question 'what are the benefits, and what
the problems, of seeking an understanding of politics in society through a focus
on decision making?'

In addition to these two threads, this course has both implicitly and explicitly
given consideration to administration. Attention has been directed to the
institutions of public administration in Britain and to the nature of the administrative function. In so doing the course has both drawn on the study of public
administration and provided an introduction to aspects of this discipline (or
as some would have it this sub-discipline of political science). In political
science there has traditionally been a division between politics and administration, and while, in the foundation year, attention was focused on the
politics dimension, in this course considerable attention has been given to
administration. In each sector a survey has been made of the institutions of
public administration, and running right through the course have been those
issues, presented at the beginning, of the extent to which administrative
institutions are involved in the political process, and of whether the instrumental theory of administration holds. Are the institutions of public administration outside the realm of politics; and can the administrative process in
Britain be regarded as a relatively mechanical process of carrying out major
policy decisions taken through the political process?

In direct conflict with what might be derived from an instrumental theory
of administration, political sociologists would postulate that those staffing the
public administration – the bureaucracy – in Britain form part of a ruling
class or ruling élite. Political sociologists in the tradition of Gaetano Mosca
have regarded the bureaucracy in modern western societies as an integral
part of a ruling class or ruling élite, and in postulating such a role for the
bureaucracy in Britain, a directly contrary point of view is being presented to

Part 4 Contents

Introduction

One aim of this course has been to stimulate and equip you to go on to investigate further topics to which you have been introduced during the course. Indeed this was stated as a general course objective:

> 1a   To become better equipped with the knowledge, abilities and skills required for formulating judgements about, and deepening knowledge of, decision making in society.

Throughout the course there has been the hope and expectation that you would be taking points further and the expectation now is that many of you will want to go on to pursue enquiries on your own. It may be that you will wish to consider and investigate some other sector such as education or employment; or you may wish to deepen your knowledge about the process of decision making, or approach British society in some other way than through sectors. Whatever your interest you will want to explore the area or topic through available material, published and even unpublished. The range of source material potentially available was outlined in Block I, Part 4, Section 2 ('The critical use of sources') but you will need to find a point of entry into the mass of material potentially available. John Simpson, the Librarian at the Open University, and P. M. Smith, an Assistant Librarian, have therefore prepared a brief introductory guide for you. Whatever your interest you will need to undertake an investigation of the literature and it is on this that they provide guidance.

This guidance we have included in pursuit of the aim of equipping you to advance your own study of decision making in Britain, but there is no intention of testing or examining your recall of this information or mastery of the skill. Indeed you would probably do well to postpone your study of this part of the block until after the examinations. But once the exams are past you will find it most rewarding – and no doubt beneficial for future courses – if you do study this guidance, and experiment with the skill of undertaking a literature search in a major library.

Section 1
The use of libraries and literature

A. E. Housman remarked in an off-moment that 'The Grizzly Bear is huge and wild. He has devoured the infant child. The infant child is not aware He has been eaten by the bear.'

In working through the course you will have discovered that the literature of decision making is also huge and wild, and the innocent student may easily be lost in it.

Can it be tamed?

The short answer is, not completely, but a systematic approach will help you to win some of the battles. Let us look at the problem in three parts:

1   Books generally
2   The formal literature of decision making
3   Primary sources

1   Books generally

The perversity of authors and publishers has ensured that books use a bewildering variety of ways to convey information. It is worth examining the parts of a book before diving into the main text, as this can save trouble and error.

Jacket. This usually contains a **blurb**, or sales plug. This is intended to praise the book but may still help to indicate its scope and purpose.

Binding or outer cover. This usually carries a **spine title** and **cover title.** These may be abbreviated and misleading. The real title is on the title page. (In pamphlets the cover may serve also as title page.)

Preliminaries.   These usually include:

> *Bastard title page.*   This carries a brief title and may name the *series* to which a book belongs.
>
> *Frontispiece.*   An illustration facing the title page.
>
> *Title page.*   The front and rear of this carry:
>
>> *Title*, in full
>> *Subtitle*, with further explanation
>> *Author's name*, qualifications, names of other works, etc., useful for gauging his standing
>> *Editor's name*
>> *Edition*
>> *Imprint*, including *place of publication, publisher's name* and *date*. The date helps to show whether the book is up-to-date. Subtract one to two years for the time taken to write and publish the book. Check also the dates of references to see how up-to-date the author's research was.

> *Preface.*   This may give the author's reasons for writing the book. It may say for what group of people the book is intended, e.g. general public, undergraduates, etc., and explain how to use the book.

> *Introduction.*   This may describe the general subject and plan of the book. It sometimes forms the first chapter of the book.

> *Table of contents.*   This lists chapters, and sometimes sections and para-

graphs with page numbers. If the book lacks an index, the table of contents is the main guide to the book.

Lists of illustrations

Text

Addenda.   Revised editions may have important material here which updates or corrects the text.

Auxiliaries.   These usually include:

Appendices.   Further material which would have cluttered the text.

Bibliography.   This may be a list of references consulted or recommended to the reader. It is usually near the end of the book, but it may be split to follow each chapter, placed in footnotes, or distributed in the text itself.

Glossary.   This defines terms used in the book or in the subject it deals with.

Footnotes.   These may explain points in the text.

Index.   Usually alphabetical, arranged letter-by-letter (e.g. *Encyclopaedia Britannica* index) or word-by-word (e.g. *Whitaker's Almanack* index). These arrangements look similar, but radically affect the positions in which entries of more than one word are placed. The index may be split into separate lists of names and subjects.

Reference books.   These usually give explicit instructions for their use and may also explain the principles upon which they have been compiled. This is particularly important in tables of statistics. For examples of difficulties in using UK official statistics, see

BRAY, J. (1970) *Decision in government*, Gollancz, and FESSEY, M. C. (1970) *Development in official economic statistics*, in Library Association, RSI Section, 18th Annual Conference, York, April 1970, *Proceedings* (1971) LA.RSIS. pp. 34–47.

2   The formal literature of decision making

After outlining the use of a single book we may look at the pitfalls of books in the mass. As the syllabus pointed out, five disciplines are involved in the course: political science, sociology, economics, geography and psychology. The literatures of these five overlap into those of the mass media, statistics, law, education, commerce, the natural sciences, technology and history. In all, most of the resources of large, general research libraries will be brought into play, as well as those of many specialized libraries and information sources. How is this to be done?

2.1   It is essential to become familiar with the use of a large library. This is difficult if you live in a remote rural area, but the services available in small local libraries and through the mail will not be enough if you wish to exploit the literature thoroughly. They must be supplemented by planned periodic visits to a large library where a good range of abstracts, indexes and bibliographies may be seen.

2.2.   If there is a printed guide to the use of the library read it and ask the library staff for help if you meet difficulties. Make sure that you understand the use of the library catalogues. These refer you from a written reference via the notation, or code giving the subject and location of the book, to the actual book on the shelves. Nearly all libraries arrange their books in classified subject order, which tends to group books on the same subject together. Browsing around the shelves where books on your special subjects are located will lead you to further useful material and sometimes also to unexpected inspiration. Informal search is important when dealing with the literature of decision making, which draws from a very wide range of disciplines and has ill-defined boundaries. The structure and terminology of the subject are unstable, which makes indexing, classification and retrieval of the literature difficult.

Many general guides to the use of libraries and literature have been written and your local librarian will be able to show you some of them. Two examples are given in the list of reference books below.

2.3   While becoming familiar with the library examine reference works such as abstracts, almanacs, atlases, bibliographies, biographical dictionaries, dictionaries, directories, encyclopaedias, gazetteers, handbooks, indexes, yearbooks, etc. A working knowledge of a moderate number of reference books will enable you to answer a surprisingly large number of questions. Your set book *Britain: an Official Handbook* is a good example of a reference book useful in a wide range of fields. Here are a few which you may find helpful:

General guides

GATES, JEAN KEY (1969) *Guide to the use of books and libraries*, 2nd edition, McGraw-Hill. Concentrates on the use of academic libraries. Examples are mainly from US libraries and literature.

LINDEN, RONALD (1965) *Books and libraries: a guide for students*, 2nd edition, Cassell. Concentrates on the use of school, college or large public libraries.

Bibliographies

Bibliographic index: a cumulative bibliography of bibliographies. 3 per year (1937 on) H. W. Wilson. Covers 1500 periodicals. Includes concealed bibliographies from monograph literature.

British national bibliography. Weekly (1950 on). Lists books published in Britain by author, title and subject.

Cumulative book index: a world list of books in the English language. Monthly (1928 on) H. W. Wilson. An author, title and subject index.

Conference proceedings

Directory of published proceedings. Quarterly (1968 on), Interdok.

Government publications. Guides and lists

Catalogue of Government publications. Annual, HMSO.

Daily List of Government publications. HMSO.

Government publications issued during . . . (monthly catalogue) HMSO.

OLLE, JAMES G. (1965) *An Introduction to British Government publications.* Association of Assistant Librarians. A simple general approach.

PEMBERTON, JOHN E. (1971) *British official publications*, Oxford, Pergamon. A detailed guide. Includes alphabetical lists of Royal Commissions, 1900–1969, and Departmental Committees, Working Parties, Tribunals of Inquiry, etc., 1900–1969.

Indexes to periodicals

British humanities index. Quarterly (1962 on). Library Association. Covers *c.* 350 periodicals including many in social sciences.

Social sciences and humanities index. Quarterly (1965 on) H. W. Wilson. Covers *c.* 200 periodicals.

Research in progress

Great Britain. Department of Education and Science. *Scientific research in British universities and colleges.* Annual. Vol. 3 covers social sciences, including research in government departments and other institutions.

Specialist sources of information

Aslib directory. 2 vols. (1968–1970). Subject guide to British organizations, including libraries, which are sources of specialized information.

Statistics

HARVEY, JOAN M. (1971) *Sources of statistics*, 2nd edition, Bingley. A thorough guide.

Theses

Dissertation abstracts. Monthly (1952 on). University Microfilms. Doctoral dissertations from 160 American universities. *Index to theses accepted for higher degrees in the universities of Great Britain and Ireland*. Annual (1950 on). Aslib. 6000 entries per year.

2.4 Having mastered these general tools you may care to examine some more specialized tools concerned with the social sciences. The guides to the literature give details of a large range of bibliographical tools which there is no space to discuss here.

Social sciences: literature guides

GRAY, RICHARD A. (comp.) (1969) *Serial bibliographies in the humanities and social sciences*, Pierian Press. Thorough. 1409 entries.

HOSELITZ, BERT F. (ed.) (1970) *A reader's guide to the social sciences*, rev. edition, Collier-Macmillan.

LEWIS, PETER R. (1960) *The literature of the social sciences: an introductory survey and guide*, Library Association. Out of date, but still useful.

MASON, JOHN BROWN (1968-9) *Research resources: annotated guides to the social sciences*, 2 vols., ABC-Clio. Vol. 2 covers official publications of US and international organizations.

WHITE, CARL M., *et al.* (1964) *Sources of information in the social sciences: a guide to the literature*, Bedminster.

Social sciences: abstracts, bibliographies, indexes and lists

ABC Pol. Sci. Advance bibliography of contents: political science and government. 8 per year (1969 on). ABC-Clio. Reproduces contents pages of 260 periodicals. Has cumulative author and subject indexes.

British Library of Political and Economic Science. *Monthly list of additions*. 1400 entries per year.

Current contents: behavioral, social and educational sciences. Weekly. ISI. Reproduces contents pages of *c.* 1100 periodicals. Useful to keep up to date, but not for retrospective search.

Index of economic articles in journals and collective volumes, 1966– (1969 on). Irwin. Continues *Index of economic journals*.

Index of economic journals 1886–1965. 5 vols. (1961–1962). Irwin. Wider range than title suggests. Continued by *Index of economic articles in journals* . . .

International bibliography of the social sciences. Annual, Unesco.

Indexes periodical articles and books. In 4 series. *Economics*. 8000 items p.a. *Political science*. 5000. *Social and cultural anthropology*. 3000. *Sociology*. 6000.

International political science abstracts. Quarterly (1951 on) Blackwell. Covers periodicals from a wider range of social sciences than the title suggests.

Keesing's contemporary archives: weekly diary of world events (1931 on). Useful to trace dates and references to more detailed primary sources.

London bibliography of the social sciences. 21 vols. (1931–1970) London School of Economics. Lists by subject the holdings of the British Library of Political and Economic Science and other London libraries.

PAIS. Bulletin of the Public Affairs Information Service. Weekly (1915 on). Indexes 30,000 items per year.

Sociological abstracts. 8 per year (1952 on). *c.* 3300 abstracts per year. Covers political sociology, public opinion, bureaucracy, etc.

Social sciences: encyclopaedia

International encyclopedia of the social sciences (1968) 17 vols., Macmillan and Free Press.

2.5   When you know your way around the library and its stock a systematic approach to literature search is needed so as to avoid wasting time in muddled hunting about. Here is an example of a generalized method.

Literature search method

Determine your **subject.** State it precisely. If you are not sure of a precise definition of the subject use **dictionaries, encyclopaedias,** including those of special subjects, **glossaries** (the terminologies of the several disciplines are not uniform), **handbooks, manuals,** or **textbooks.**

Determine the **time scope** of the search. How far back will it be useful to go?

How **intensive** should the search be? How long shall it take? Shall it range outside the library to other sources? Indexes vary a good deal in quality. To avoid missing useful items it is advisable to check **broader subjects** which contain the subject sought, **narrower subjects** which are contained in the subject sought, **allied subjects** which have points in common with the subject sought.

Analyse the subject into its **aspects.** Pursue the literature of each aspect. As you search, record **sources searched, terms** checked in the sources, **period** covered. Check the quality of the books you consult, e.g. check a subject you know. Is it fully explained? Biased? Too popular?

Are the bibliographies sound and up to date? If you want an introduction to the subject look for **textbooks, handbooks** or **monographs.** Determine the **subject headings** involved.

Review the headings searched with each tool used.

Check the **subject index** to the **library catalogue.**

Check the **classified catalogue** (if any) under the numbers found in the subject index.

Check the **classified list of periodicals** (if any).

Check the **shelves** for items found.

Browse **adjacent shelves** for allied subjects.

If no document found satisfies your requirements begin a search of bibliographical tools. As you come to each tool for the first time, read the **foreword** and **instructions to the user.**

Record references found in a uniform way.

Use standard abbreviations. Do not invent your own. If in doubt, do not abbreviate.

Record each reference on a separate card or slip, to aid sorting.

Reference format

    Author.

    Title in full.

    Source, e.g. Periodical title in standard abbreviated form.

    Volume number, **part** number, **date, page** numbers.

    Publisher, if a book.

    Place of publication, if obscure.

    Notes or abstracts, if wanted.

    Keywords, if wanted.

Check **Literature guides**
　　　Bibliographies
　　　Catalogues

Look for **review articles.** Check the periodicals index for titles containing phrases such as:

　　　Advances in . . .
　　　Annual reports on . . .
　　　Annual review of . . .
　　　. . . Reviews
　　　International review of . . .
　　　Progress in . . .
　　　Recent advances in . . .
　　　Recent progress in . . .
　　　Reports on . . .
　　　Reviews of . . .
　　　Survey of . . .
　　　Symposium on . . .
　　　Yearbook of . . .

These may contain bibliographies.

Check **guides to periodicals** to discover specialist periodicals.

Check **indexes to periodicals** and **abstracts.** Work backwards from current issues. This reaches later work first and may disclose bibliographies. Look for **cumulated indexes.** Search the most important source first.

Check **other works by the authors of your selected references** and **works cited in those references.** These will in turn provide a further set of citations which you may find worth following up.

Check **corporate authors' other publications.**

Check **Directories**
　　　Indexes to reports
　　　Monographs
　　　Theses
　　　Conference proceedings
　　　Foreign literature
　　　Research reports
　　　Other sources of information, e.g.
　　　　　Special libraries
　　　　　Information bureaux
　　　　　Societies
　　　　　Trade associations
　　　　　Government departments

Keep up to date. Scan **current periodicals, news magazines, newspapers.**

Edit your discovered references into a useful systematic order.

3   Primary sources

These have already been discussed in Block I, pp. 129–54. Some of the items included in the Block III Dossier on agriculture have been reproduced from primary sources and item 18 lists some documents which illustrate an interesting point. Most of them are secondary sources for the subjects of which they treat. They are all, however, primary sources for the study of 'media sources of information used by farmers . . .'.

Use of the primary sources is made more difficult by the wide range of forms which they take. These now include films, video tapes, audio tapes, gramophone records, data banks on magnetic tape or disc which can be approached only through a computer system, computer output on microfiche, ultrafiche (3360 pages on a transparency $6'' \times 4''$), etc. They can be used only with the aid of special equipment for listening, viewing or manipulation. Their bibliographical control is much weaker than that of the printed media, so they are hard to trace and locate.

Some sources may be unpublished, informally circulated or suppressed (decision makers do not usually advertise their mistakes deliberately).

How may these elusive sources be discovered?

Some are listed in the literature guides to the social sciences. More will be mentioned in the sources turned up during literature searches. Other researchers in the field will be able to help and the staff of specialized libraries and information sources may have personal contacts with the custodians of primary sources which can save a great deal of frustrating search. This is akin to the 'invisible colleges' in which researchers know their fellows throughout the world, attend conferences, and exchange information in unpublished form. There is little likelihood of such informal systems being replaced by formal, widely available services in the near future.

There is still a great deal of research to be done on the literature needs of social scientists. BRITTAIN, J. M. (1970) *Information and its users: a review with special reference to the social sciences*, Bath University Press and Oriel, discusses the problems presented by the nature of the literature of the social sciences and the difficulties encountered by various groups of users working with it.

But this is long term work. Your research will have to be done with the literature and library services as they presently exist.

As in many other fields, search becomes easier as you come to know what to look for. Serendipity (the knack of discovering things by accident) begins to function as you notice useful items not directly concerned with your systematic searches. During your regular scanning of newspapers and political and social weeklies, items which you would previously have passed over clamour for your attention. You will be getting the feel of literature search.

If you are not able to spend long periods in a large library you may feel that you are less fortunate than a student resident in a university with a well stocked library at hand. To some extent this is true, but the disadvantage can be largely overcome.

Use of a library may be of two kinds. Firstly, active search, as discussed earlier. Secondly, a more passive use – the reading of the material discovered or merely the reading of portions of texts recommended by a tutor. Some undergraduates use libraries only in this passive way and, even though they spend many hours in a library, they may never learn to use it properly or to make their own approach to the literature.

Use your time in libraries for constructive work with the literature and not in reading items which you can obtain for use at home. This will require careful advance planning, but once you have acquired the habit of intensive literature search you will find it especially helpful as your researches extend to specialist sources around the country. No library is self-sufficient. When you are able to use a number of sources effectively you will have a key to the literature of your subject which could not be acquired by the use of a single library, no matter how large.

Literature search is demanding work, and it is tempting to halt after a respectable amount of published material has been located and obtained.

As has been mentioned earlier, the primary sources of decision making range far wider than published books and periodicals. A search which did not include the mass media such as television and radio would be less than adequate. You will have to venture into many such areas where the maps are poor and the signposts misleading, so do not hesitate to consult librarians, archivists and information officers as you work with their documents. They are far more than guardians or custodians and take pleasure in seeing their stocks being exploited effectively in the pursuit of information.

If you have occasion to use a specialist library belonging to an organization such as a trade union, a learned society or a firm, please remember that its primary function is to serve the organization which set it up, and that organization has first call upon its resources. However, even the most hard-pressed librarian welcomes the courteous and appreciative student. Gaining knowledge of the literature, though exacting work, presents some of the challenges of detective work. It also brings pleasure and the friendship of other workers with the literature, both students and librarians. Good hunting.

Notes

Notes

BAT CAN'T SLEEP

CARLY GLEDHILL

Macmillan Children's Books

Bat can't sleep.
She isn't like other bats.

They like to sleep during the day. But Bat is too excited!